The Raising of a Rebel

12 Turning Points from a Child of Alcoholics

Memoir of Glenn Eugene Odom

Written by Tonya Eberhart

The Raising of a Rebel

Published by Bold Brand Publishing, LLC
Copyright © 2021 Tonya Eberhart
All rights reserved.
ISBN: 978-0-578-87941-3

DEDICATION

Cheryl Odom:
For supporting me in my darkest times, and encouraging me to make better decisions. You stood behind me even when I wasn't myself, and you have never wavered in your love and support. I'll always remember the love and care you showed for my Daddy, too. I'm proud to call you my wife.

Dr. Herbert Robinson:
For always being there for me. Thank you for having a positive impact on my life. You always inspired me to get back on the right path, even when I would detour occasionally. There isn't one impressionable part of my life that you didn't impact.

Ford Phillips:
Thank you for your faith in my talent, and all those rides home after practice and games. I can't remember you ever criticizing me. When you announced that I might be on the Varsity team in the 9th grade, it made me work even harder. You were a great coach, and I still think about you a lot.

Aunt Ethel:
You were my rock. I will always be in awe of your tireless efforts to take care of me, Janet, Harold, and Ronald. You provided me with a safe home and incredible food on the table at a time when I needed

it most. Were it not for you, this book would not even be possible.

Edgar & Gaynelle Odom:
You allowed me to work in your chicken house to make money and always welcomed me into your home. The day Edgar sold me the 1957 Ford Custom 300 was a moment I'll never forget. It was probably the most popular car around among teenagers, and it gave me confidence and made me feel that I had accomplished something.

Morris Martin:
You taught me the correct way to shoot a basketball, helped me put up my first goal, and provided me with transportation when I needed it. You even hitchhiked to the gym in Dawsonville with me on occasion, and helped my daughter learn to ride her first bicycle.

My Teammates:
Thank you to all of my basketball teammates who did most of the work while I got most of the glory. No one succeeds alone, and the recognition I received would not have been possible without the entire team's efforts.

My Classmates:
Thank you for accepting me and making me feel supported even though many of you knew my struggles. Every person I encountered was especially kind, and that's almost impossible for anyone to say

about their high school years. I am grateful to have been surrounded by such great people.

Daryl & Rodney Robinson:
Neither of you ever looked down on me, even when I messed up. Thank you, Daryl, for saving the write-ups from my basketball days. That was an unexpected and kind gesture that I'll never forget. You have both been incredibly supportive throughout many years of friendship.

Pete & Linda Bearden
You're not only my friends, but you've been like family to me. We've shared a lot of memories, both personal and business related. We've helped each other at times throughout the years, and I have always known that I could count on your friendship. I can't imagine not having you both in my life.

Jimmy Tatum
You've been a true friend since elementary school. We have never had a cross word, even when you knew I was making bad choices. There was one time during our lives when we didn't see each other for almost a decade, and we picked right back up where we left off when we reconnected. Thank you for being there.

Clyde Wilson
You have also been a true friend since first grade, and like Jimmy, we have never had a cross word. We've seen many of life's ups and downs together.

You have the kindest heart of anyone I know, and you've helped me through some tough situations. I'm proud to know that we've remained friends throughout all these years.

Sherri Raines
I watched you grow up alongside Tonya & Michael, and recall some beautiful memories from those days. You're a caring person with a huge heart, and I always wish the very best for you. Your Daddy will always have a special place in my heart, and you will always be my baby sister.

Roger Slaton
We had many years of Park & Rec basketball together, which is where we first became good friends. You have always had my best interest in mind and treated me with respect, even when I was at my lowest. I appreciate your friendship and loyalty all these years.

Kay Gearhart:
I can't imagine a more incredible mother to our children. You and I bonded out of love, respect, and painful pasts. When we became parents at such a young age, it turned out to be one of the greatest accomplishments in my life, despite my immature view at the time. We went through 'the best of times' and 'the worst of times' together, and I credit you for so many positive things that shape me to this day. I respect you tremendously, and always wish the best for you.

Michael Odom:
I've always been proud of you, son. You worked hard to become a basketball player like me, except I was 5'10" and you were 6'4", and you started on the varsity team as a freshman. I can't describe the feeling of watching you from the stands. I believe you were just a few points shy of breaking the title of the most points scored at Dawson County High School during your time there. I still have some of your game videos. We've had some turbulent moments between us, but I will always love you.

Tonya Eberhart:
You've always made me proud. During your basketball days, I watched you knock the bottom out of it many times. You were such a great shooter, and I was so excited and proud the day I saw your first musical play. Throughout all the years, you always seemed to know the answers, even if I didn't listen. You were, and still are, the matriarch of our family. You were right when you said, "It's all about choices." I can't express the gratitude I feel for your time to write this book.

FOREWORD

Words spoken are but a vapor. But written, they are captured for all time. I can't explain why, but that thought was on my mind the day I called my Dad and approached him with the idea of writing his story. First, it's an incredible story. Incredibly sad, funny, tragic...and real. Second, it's a story I want my children and future grandchildren to know. In all its glory and its pain.

When I first approached him with the idea of this book, it was the Spring of 2019. I was in Columbus, Ohio at the time, and I called him and said, "Dad, I have an idea." Now, to those who know me well, that could create a slightly alarming feeling. I have never been known for small ideas.

When I told him that I wanted to write his memoir, I couldn't even hear crickets through the phone line for about eight seconds. Now, to those of you who know my Dad well, you'd know silence isn't one of his primary traits. When he finally spoke, his voice was tight, and I could envision him slumping his shoulders and lifting his furrowed brow as he spoke these words: *"What did I do to deserve a book?"* Immediately, I knew it was something that had to happen.

My Dad's story actually begins long before his birth in 1947. He was born into a moonshine family, whose heritage dates back generations. And as we all know, with moonshine came the fast cars, and with fast cars came the fast drivers. This led to the beginnings of the auto racing industry. Early racing icons such as Lloyd Seay, Roy Hall, Gober Sosebee, Bernard Long and Raymond Parks helped to launch a sport that grew from necessity into entertainment.

The moonshine industry spawned an entire legacy for the area, and now, Dawsonville boasts of six different Daytona winners. That includes modern day racing icons Bill Elliott and his son, Chase Elliott.

Lloyd Seay was the first man from Dawsonville to win what was called the National Stock Car Championship in 1941. He was also well known in the liquor business in Atlanta, and famous for frequently driving with his car up on two wheels. Most folks around Dawsonville who knew him and saw him race will tell you that he's the best driver they've ever seen.

Although I'd love to go on about the moonshine and racing industry (that's for another book), it's actually the foundation for the story you're about to read. The moonshine industry's tentacles run deep and wide, and bring both fortune and misfortune to this story and many others.

I can only share with you the experiences I have witnessed as a product of the profession that began so long ago. As you can imagine, it was a turbulent journey at times. As a child, you either don't notice the dysfunction swirling around you, or you think it's normal. But as you grow in age and experience, you come into your own awakening. Little by little, truths are revealed, and you realize exactly who you are and where you come from.

I can tell you thousands of amazing memories I have about my Dad, but here are a few that stand out, and define the complex human being that is about to be unveiled throughout these pages.

I recall the day Dad came home from work with two sets of boxing gloves. Me and my brother, Michael, used to fight all the time. And I mean the Evander Holyfield and Mike Tyson style of fighting. My parents had grown so sick of it, that Dad thought it was time for the final round. So, we both put on gloves, and fought until blood was drawn. I'm sure he did it to teach us that we were solely responsible for putting an end to it.

I remember the excitement of receiving my first basketball around the age of four. Dad put up a goal beside the house, and I shot for hours upon hours, dreaming of the day I could shoot as good as Dad. Whenever he did let me win an occasional game of horse, I was elated. Basketball became a real passion for me, and he even coached me in my elementary school years a couple of times.

Dad gave us a list of chores every day, and on Saturdays, we were tasked with picking up pine cones and limbs and raking billions of pine needles from the yard. I hated those mornings, and would sneak into the house and call my Aunt Ethel. I asked her to come and get me, and within thirty minutes, she showed up in the driveway. I don't think Dad ever grew wise to that one.

When he took the trash to the city dump on the weekends, I begged to go, and talked him into letting me drive down the long gravel road to the dump. We often went to the Dawsonville Pool Room, Looper's Supermarket, or the Tasty Freeze during our errands.

Almost every Sunday for several summers, we canoed or tubed down the Etowah or Amicalola River. My Dad had concocted an inner tube that he called 'The Cadillac', which had one big truck tube for a seat, and two smaller ones (one attached as a head support, and one to prop up his feet). Then he attached yet another tube to his, which contained a cooler. It was impressive, I must say.

Once when Michael and I were canoeing with Dad, we passed several people who were sunbathing nude along the riverbank. This was at an area of the river where most people had to stop and carry the canoes over rocks because it was too steep and narrow to go down. Luckily, the nudists put their clothes on before we reached the rocks. That was a thrilling day for a young kid.

I even remember the first time I got involved in the liquor business. *Hold on, it's not what you think.* Dad came home with what seemed like hundreds of milk jugs, and Mom would clean them and run a rope through the handle of about 25 of them at a time. They made a large cluster that looked like grapes, and whenever they moved, the empty jugs made a sound just like thunder.

Dad would give us each a string full of them, and tell us to run outside and put them in the smokehouse. There were only two rules. We had to wait until dark so no one would see us, and we had to run fast. Well, that clandestine job made us giggle with delight, and we were disappointed when we ran out of jugs.

Those are just a few of the fond memories I recall from early childhood. *And then things started to change.* When Mom and Dad got divorced, I began to realize the depth of dysfunction, and the reality of change hit like a ton of bricks. All of a sudden, Dad began showing up late for major events. He partied all the time, and introduced me to several girlfriends over the next few years, few of whom lasted much longer than the introduction.

My memories of the next thirty plus years are mixed with frustration, pity, love, and tragedy. It was a wild ride, and even though I was away from home during most of it, I was pulled back into the chaos on a regular basis when things got really bad, which was quite often in those days.

During his first bad car accident, I was in Panama City, Florida. I received a call from home, and the situation appeared bleak. Dad had multiple injuries, and they weren't sure he would survive. I called my good friend, Diana, whom I'd met at Gainesville Junior College, and told her what had happened. Diana was Bill Elliott's assistant at the time. She called Bill and Ron, who was Bill's pilot, and asked if Ron could fly the plane down to Panama City to pick me up and bring me home.

I had no idea she was making the call, and I was humbled and grateful that someone would do that for me. Ron flew me to a regional airport in Gainesville, Georgia, through heavy rain, and I was taken straight to the hospital when we landed. Dad's head was so swollen that he was hardly recognizable, and all he could do was whisper. His friend was in a coma, and getting ready for brain surgery. They were both extremely lucky to survive. I extend a debt of gratitude to Diana, Bill, and Ron for their extreme kindness during that time.

Over the next several years, the chaos continued, despite that tragic experience. By this time, I had moved to Columbus, Ohio. One Mother's Day weekend, I received word from home that Dad had been on another bender for weeks, and someone had finally talked him into going to the Emergency

Room. After they checked him in, they sent him to Laurelwood, a dry out facility in Gainesville. They could only hold him for 48 hours, though, and I was communicating several times a day with Dad and his counselor, trying to find a longer-term rehab facility that he could attend as soon as he was released. I knew that if he went straight back home, the nightmare would continue, so I was forced to deal with another situation that demanded immediate attention.

I remember being on the phone with the counselor, and we were discussing the fact that Dad had to pass a phone screen interview before he could transfer into another facility. I wasn't sure he could do that, because he was still showing signs of confusion and paranoia. He kept insisting to me that there was a painting of a bull on the wall, and its eyes were following him all around the facility. He was convinced that he was being watched by every animate (and inanimate) object that he passed. And, of course, they were listening to every word, too, so occasionally his voice would drop to a whisper.

I was still hopeful that he could get through that interview, at least until the counselor said, "Do you know what name your Dad used when he checked in?" I replied that I didn't. There was a slight pause, followed by, *"He checked himself in as Jesus Christ"*.

Then there was the time he came down to Florida with a friend of his to visit for a few days. One afternoon I came home from work to find the two of them chatting upstairs with two women they had met at a strip club the night before. I respectfully suggested that they all go out to dinner, and ushered them out as quickly as possible. I never let him forget that one.

In fact, there wasn't much that I ever let Dad forget. Whenever he was misbehaving, all someone had to do was threaten to call me, and he would at least curb his behavior momentarily. He hated it when I called him to the carpet, but he always listened respectfully. Even if he didn't change a thing.

During one of my long lectures on how he should be living his life, I recall telling him, *"Dad, it's all about choices."* For some reason, that statement has resonated all these years later. If you ask him what he remembers most about all the unwanted advice I gave him over the years, I'm sure that's the phrase that he will repeat. Probably because it's an inescapable truth.

I'll leave you with this story, which actually became my most viewed blog post in 2015. And, you guessed it, it was about my Dad. Ironically, it was also posted on April Fool's Day, but it actually happened. Every word of it.

Even more strange, I learned right before publishing this book that April 1, 1986 was the day that Dad went into treatment for the first time. Upon check-in, they asked him, "Mr. Odom, how are you doing today?", to which he replied, "Well, I guess I'm your April Fool addict". It's funny how things come full circle.

Blog Post on BrandFaceStar.com
April 1, 2015

So many interesting stories throughout my adulthood have begun with the words, "My Dad was visiting last week and..."

Well, it happened again. And this time I couldn't resist sharing possibly the strangest branding conversation ever.

My Dad was visiting last week and...we were headed back to Columbus after spending the day in Cincinnati watching my son play volleyball. My Dad was taking note of the roadside corn and soybean fields when he blurted out, "Hey honey, a few years ago I came up with a great idea and I can't believe no one has done it yet". [*Oh no*]

"You know those billboards that are v-shaped, the ones that have the platforms in between them? Did you know that those platform areas are bigger than some apartments? And they have electricity at those things." [*I can only imagine where he's going with this*] "Don't you think some homeless people would have figured that out by now? I mean...they could literally live on that platform. It has sides already, so they would just need to add a roof. And with electricity, they could have heat." [*Trust me, it gets stranger*]

He continues, "If you really think about it, you could live there pretty comfortably [*by whose definition?*] and no one would know. With electricity, you could cook steaks [*steaks?!*], even have a TV and air conditioning." [*WTH?!*]

So, of course my creative curiosity gets the best of me and (God help me) I begin to fuel the flame by peppering him with questions. "Seriously? An air conditioning unit?", I asked. [*Of all the questions, I chose to focus on that?*] "How would you get it up there?" Without hesitation, he replied with a detailed, technical description of a pulley system.

As we continued to drive up the interstate, he was quite disappointed that there were no v-shaped billboards to show me. He did, however, find a few with a narrow platform in between the two parallel sides, and mentioned that even the space between those was actually much larger than it looked. [*Now we're in too deep to back out*]

So, I asked the question you're probably all thinking, too. "Dad, what would you do for a bathroom?" Now, you'd think I was expecting the obvious answer (climb down and use the great outdoors), but I knew better than to expect the expected. He continues, with frightening nonchalance, "You see, you don't want to have to climb down every time you've gotta go. So, you cut a hole in the platform and just use it like an outhouse" [*OK, gotta give him that*]. Or [*brace yourself*] you could cut off the top of one of those big post cylinders that run up the side, use the bathroom in those, and it would take you literally five years to fill it up". [*I'm wondering at this point whether I'm having an out of body experience*].

Over the next hour [*kid you not*], we discussed the pros and cons of living in a billboard. No mortgage, no electric bill, no taxes, no pesky visitors. The different materials (and even weight limit) the pulley system could accommodate. And the fact that fresh water might be the only real challenge. We even discussed the added benefit of the amazing view (depending on location, of course). I think we stopped just shy of home decor.

We pondered the need for the sign company to periodically access the platform to change the sign and how frequently that might take place. We debated the square footage of the platform and exactly how much space constitutes 'enough room to live comfortably'.

Then I stepped in with both feet. I couldn't help myself. I said, "You could be 'Billboard Gene'. I could get you so much press coverage." I could already envision the streaming video, selling attraction tickets like they do for the Swiss Family Robinson

Treehouse...plus t-shirts, hot plates and toilet seats with the 'Billboard Gene' logo. Even a fashion empire featuring his signature jeans, appropriately named 'Billboard Genes' with multiple velcro-flapped pockets for securing items during 'the climb'.

As we neared the end of the conversation, he added (in an almost too serious tone), "If I'm ever homeless, now you know where to find me".

My friends, it's precisely moments like this when you know... 1) where your creativity comes from and 2) that branding is what you were born to do.

Indeed, my Dad has brought great adventures into my life. He has taught me to be tough, persistent, and above all, to dream big. He has taught me the positive side of 'rebel'.

On the flip side, regardless of the turbulence and turmoil, we have survived another day. And as they say in Alcoholics Anonymous, we take it one day at a time. What my Dad doesn't realize is that beyond the chaos, there was a distinct foundation of love. Through all the craziness, I always knew I was loved. I always knew my Dad would be there. And he knew that I would, too.

It hasn't always been pretty, but it's been real. Throughout this story, I hope you will grow to understand the essence of the man behind the mayhem. He is wickedly funny, genuinely inspiring, and has a heart large enough to fill a stadium. And I am insanely proud to call him my Dad.

So, Dad, my answer to your question, "What did I do to deserve a book?", is...*everything*. Everything you have suffered. Everything you have sacrificed. Everything you have overcome. Every stumble. Every success. Every memory.

The truth is, everyone deserves a book. We all have a story to tell, and to someone, it's exactly the story they need to hear. In the pages ahead, I hope you find something that you need to hear.

Yes, words spoken are but a vapor, and the ability to capture them for all time in this book is an honor and a pleasure.

I love you, Dad.

– Tonya

INTRODUCTION

When Tonya first approached me about writing this book, I was actually a little shocked. Although I could hear the excitement in her voice, a thousand thoughts immediately swirled through my head. I was trying to grasp what that would mean.

Would people really care? And if they didn't, would that be OK? Would I make people mad? Would I hurt someone's feelings? And, finally...would I tell *all*? I can promise you that at this very moment (even if you are reading this years after the date of publication), I am probably still considering some of those questions. I am still wondering if I made the right decisions, used the right words, or shared more than I should have.

The biggest question I considered was the *purpose* of the book. Many of you may think it to be self-serving, and I must be honest and say that it does feel good to have a book written about me. But that's only part of the equation. It occurred to me almost instantly that it would provide an opportunity for me to do two things. To shed a light on the reasons why I made some of the choices I made, and to apologize to those I have hurt in doing so.

In this book, you'll witness my struggles, my mistakes, and a few victories I have been blessed with along the way. Above all, I'd like to let you know in advance that you're going to hear some unpleasant and controversial things. I don't expect you to agree with them, or condone my decisions. I simply ask that you grant me some grace and understanding in sharing the events and experiences that I feel have shaped me.

I have made an honest effort to recall the details to the best of my ability. Some of the events may be slightly out of order, and I may have missed some fine points along the way, but the spirit of the story is intact, and expressed with the best of intentions.

For those of you who are concerned about me sharing too much, we have consciously elected to protect the innocent (*and the guilty*). For that reason, there are very few names throughout the book. So, if your name wasn't mentioned, please don't take that personally. It was done simply to protect and respect you. *And perhaps keep you out of the news.*

As Tonya says, "It's all about choices." And although I can't turn back time and stand at those same crossroads again, I'm hopeful that something in this book will help *you* take a step in the right direction. The ability to share my story is a true gift, and I only hope that those who have crossed my path will have a greater understanding. To those in my life who have been harmed by those choices, please know that I am sincere when I say that was never my intention.

Above all, I am honored to have this book written about my life. It has been quite a journey, complete with resurrected memories, lots of laughs, and countless tears. Looking back can be hard. But looking inside is an awakening.

– Gene

CHAPTERS

CHAPTER 1:
Hard & Humble Beginnings

If we could see into the future, it would be empowering. But how many of us would choose to bypass life with just one glimpse through the keyhole? If I could have seen into my younger years, I might well have opted out. If I had known of the impending pain and chaos, I hope that few would have blamed me for such a choice.

I was born on December 10, 1947, in a little rock house just off the square in Dahlonega, Georgia. My Mama was just 16 years old, and my Daddy was 19. The physician was Doc Howard, my Grandpa Ed's good friend. That rock house still stands today, next to the movie theatre where I saw the first movie that I remember, *Creatures of the Black Lagoon*.

I don't remember a lot from my early childhood, mostly just scattered memories, some more vivid than others. Four years after I was born, my sister, Janet, came along. I find it strange that I scarcely have a memory of her until adulthood. Looking back, I'm certain my focus on survival and self-preservation was to blame for the omissions.

People have told me that I had immense energy, and that I was a loving child. They told me I had a wooden pony with four wheels and a long mane made of rope or yarn, and that I must have pushed it hundreds of miles.

When I was a little over two years old, we were headed to watch a movie at the Holly Theatre in Dahlonega. I was in the front seat between Daddy and my cousin, Carolyn, but I wasn't happy about it. I insisted that I wanted the spot near the door. Daddy gave in, and allowed me to sit by the door because he knew I liked to see out the window. In that car, the door handles pushed downward to open, and I apparently pushed down on the handle and was suddenly pulled out the door almost as though someone had reached in and grabbed me. Carolyn says I was wearing a red shirt that day, and I flew out the door just like a little redbird.

Daddy tried to stop the car quickly, but the brakes were no good, and he had to gear it down in order to stop it. Mama and my Aunt Ailene were in the back seat, and were so frightened that they practically jumped into the front seat. Carolyn recalls this story in vivid detail, and says she will never forget the image of me, scraped up and bleeding, but running as fast as my little legs would move, trying to catch up with the car. I was screaming over and over, "Daddy, don't leave me!".

They took me to Doc Howard's office and painted me from head to toe with mercurochrome, and we went on to the theatre. Strangely, I don't remember this incident at all.

The earliest memory I do have from my childhood was attending Grandpa Ed's funeral. He was my paternal grandfather, who was known to stay drunk most of the time. He died at the age of 68. He and my grandmother, Bertie, had ten children, one of whom was my Dad. Bertie died of pneumonia just six months after the birth of twins, which left the older daughters to raise the younger ones. Some of the children would say that, although Ed drank consistently, when the time came to harvest the crops, he would strap to the mules and become the hardest worker in the fields.

I recall traveling to his funeral, when Mama & Daddy stopped at a Pure Oil station to buy a Coca Cola to pour over the windshield to clean it, which was sometimes done in those days. They were drinking blackberry wine on the drive, passing it back and forth in the front seat. They handed the wine back to me and let me drink it. They laughed about it, and passed it back to me two or three times. I remember having a difficult time standing up, as I wavered underneath the funeral tent. I was only three or four years old.

During my early childhood, we weren't really settled down anywhere. After Grandpa Ed died, we moved in with my maternal grandparents, Winnie and Paul. Mama and Daddy left us there while they went to work at the still. They were sometimes gone for weeks or months at a time.

Mama cooked for the workers and Daddy did a multitude of things, but mostly ran the liquor. He was a legend in his time, one of the fastest liquor runners around (on foot). He lived by the moonshiner's code. You kept your word, and never ratted on anyone, regardless of the circumstance or consequence. Moonshine was the family business, and it was all he knew.

I have several memories from Paul and Winnie's house. We raised hogs and slaughtered them. The next morning after a slaughter, we'd have tenderloin for breakfast, and even though the trauma of the event was still fresh on my mind, the tenderloin was such a treat, and my elation at having really good food overcame the sadness of the circumstances.

I vividly remember my Mama's brother, Clarence. He ran with a rough crowd, and was known for fighting and shooting his rifle with great precision. In fact, he would walk across the road from the house and stick ten matches into the dirt, with the red flammable tip upward. Then he'd sit on the porch in an old wooden chair and shoot across the road at them. He could actually strike the matches with a bullet and a flame would erupt. The most fascinating thing was that the matches were still standing.

Clarence loved to hunt and fish, and he also helped make liquor to earn a living. He was known for a quick temper and violent nature, especially when he was drinking. He once attacked a man at a local beer joint in Dawsonville and sent them to the hospital for 250 stitches. He shot yet another man between the eyes and blinded him for life after being accused of flirting with the man's girlfriend. After the shooting, Clarence came home and said, "I've shot a man and I think I've killed him".

Violence continued to follow him, and Clarence was shot in the chest five times and murdered by his girlfriend's brother when he was just twenty years old. No one ever really knew why he was killed. The family laid his body at home for two days before he was buried. It was summertime, and there were fans running to take the edge off the heat and keep down the smell of death. It was an especially sad time for Mama and her other siblings. I was only nine, so I understood that he was dead, but I didn't comprehend much more than that.

Paul worked at a sawmill just two miles from home and walked to work. He would come in from work and head to the still with his mule and sled. He used the sled for carrying sugar into the still, and hauling the liquor out. One evening in 1957, he didn't return home from the still. His mule was waiting on him at the site, and he was found dead from what appeared to be natural causes. That was when Winnie came to live with us.

At that time, there were eight people living in that small cabin, including Mama's brother, sister and brother-in-law. And then there was Winnie, my grandmother. She became mentally unstable after Paul's death. Though I don't recall witnessing the event, this story was recited to me multiple times. Mama was washing dishes one night when Winnie approached her from behind with a butcher knife held high over her head. She was about to stab Mama when her brother-in-law grabbed Winnie's hand and stopped her. That's when she was sent to Milledgeville, a nearby psychiatric ward. She spent ten years there, and was later moved to an old hospital in Cumming, where she eventually passed away. Today, that hospital is a convalescent home.

I recall riding the bus to school some days, and walking through the woods to get there on others. My bus at the time was an old panel truck that only carried ten to fifteen kids. One day my bus driver accidentally ran over four of my new puppies at the same time. I was so sad, and it seemed as though I was the only one who was really bothered by it.

A few years later, another of our dogs had eight puppies. Daddy put them all in a sack and tied it up. Then we drove to Cumming and stopped beside a bridge. He made me get out of the car and toss the sack into the river below. As cruel as it seems, back then it's just how many people did things. But that moment has stayed with me throughout my life. Looking back, it would foreshadow a feeling of isolation and loneliness that would rear its head frequently.

I showed up early for school many days to help Miss Hattie Grace, my teacher, start a fire for the classroom. I was in the 1st grade at Lumpkin Campground Elementary School. I don't recall much about this period of time, but in the first grade, Mama actually attended school alongside me for a few months. She had not gone to school as a child, and she was hoping to learn how to read and write.

I didn't realize at the time how unconventional it was to have my Mama in the same classroom. She didn't attend school too long, though, because all she ever learned was how to write her name. Until the day she died, she could not read or write. Though this might seem debilitating, it was actually a testament to her because there are very few people who ever knew that she was illiterate.

When I reminisce on those early school years, they represent the only sense of childhood innocence that I can recall. I fondly remember racing around during recess with a piece of notebook paper taped to my chest with a number on it. I swear, we'd run the whole recess. I was a decent student then, who wanted to please perhaps more than anything else. And there was one person who would be introduced into my life at this time whom I would try harder than anyone to please. He was my principal, and his name was Herbert Robinson.

In the 3rd grade, Herbert caught me smoking. Back then, if you had a note from your Daddy, you could smoke at school, even as early as the 2nd grade. There was a dedicated place in the woods next to the school for kids to smoke. I succumbed to peer pressure to join some of the other kids to smoke, but I didn't have a permit. After I smoked, I picked up a handful of pine needles and chewed on them, hoping to disguise the smell of smoke on my breath.

That was the first day I ever smoked a cigarette, and Herbert caught me. I was late coming back from recess, and he stopped me and said, "Gene, I'm gonna have to whip you. You know what happens when you break the rules. I have to whip anyone who's caught smoking without a note." He whipped me in front of the whole class, so hard that it lifted me up off the ground. Tears welled in my eyes, and I was hurt and embarrassed. But I never smoked at school again.

The following year, I began attending Dawson County Elementary as a 4th grader. Just a few weeks into the school year, Herbert called me out of class to talk with me. As we walked down the hallway together, with his hand on my shoulder, he told me he was taking me back to the 3rd grade. I remember asking him, "But, what about all my friends?" In his gentle, fatherly voice, he said, "Don't worry son, you'll do better." At that moment, I felt assured that he was doing the right thing, and he was. He must have been told that I wasn't advanced enough.

Herbert Robinson impacted my life in so many ways. I recall so much about him, although I really didn't spend that much time in his presence. He was such an eloquent speaker. You could hear a pin drop in the room every time he spoke. You'd listen to every word. His Florsheim shoes were always perfectly shined. He almost looked like God walking down the hall. As long as he was around, I did not want to step out of line. A decade later, he would continue to be a major source of inspiration for me to become the first family member to graduate from high school.

Outside of my days at school, I remember Daddy being gone a lot. I do recall feeling mostly 'okay' about Mama in those early years. However, there were times when I was definitely afraid of her, and wondered if she was headed for the same fate as Winnie. Of course, this was before their drinking began to get heavier and change the course of the future for us all.

In hindsight, I know we were very poor, though I didn't realize it at the time. Fifty years later, I was talking with Mama at her kitchen table, complaining about money. She slammed her fist on the table, and said "Hell fire, son. You don't know what poor is. It's watching out your bedroom window when it's fifteen degrees outside and there's snow on the ground. You're watching the pigs and waiting for one of them to dig up a sweet potato from last spring, and when it does, you go out there and take it from the pig. Then take it to the fireplace and cook it. That's what poor is."

CHAPTER 2:
The Falsely Prosperous Years

Daddy had been working on a still on Moreland Avenue in Atlanta. He was making 300 gallons of liquor a day. He ran the entire still by himself, because he could get double the pay. When I was out of middle school for Christmas break, he sent for me to help him. The job was so rigorous that he would sometimes have to stay up 18-20 hours a day just to get it done.

My task was to jar the liquor. It was like an assembly line. While each jar was filling with liquor, I was removing a lid from the next jar, and closing the lid on yet another. There were 12 jars to a case, and when I had filled a case, I had to pick them up and stack the boxes of jars in the corner for the runner to come pick them up. I also did other things to help out, like carrying 100 pound bags of sugar into the basement, which allowed Daddy to stay with the liquor and make sure production didn't drop. We'd pick up the 100 pound sacks, cut open the top, and tilt them over into boxes measuring 4'x4'x4' where the mash was made.

When it was time for me to go back to school, Daddy took me to Sears Roebuck on Ponce de Leon Avenue in Atlanta, the biggest Sears store in the country at the time. When we walked in, he told me, "You can have anything in here that you want, son." I was elated. And immediately, a burgundy colored moped in the front store window caught my eye. It was $189.00. The speedometer showed a top speed of 45 miles per hour. With stars in my eyes, I watched as Daddy went up to the counter and paid for it. We put it in the trunk and headed back to the still.

I wanted to crank it so badly, but Daddy said, "Let's don't crank it yet. Somebody might hear it. Wait until we fire the still up tonight." That night, as soon as the still started running, I cranked the moped. I was in heaven. I was so excited, I'd run over to the moped between jarring cases of liquor and crank it. Daddy didn't say anything. He just grinned.

After he heard it running, he realized it wasn't too loud after all, so the next day he let me take it outside and ride it around the house. I swear, I wore a trail that was six inches deep around the still. This was my first taste of instant gratification on a big level.

Daddy made enough money in six months to buy land, build a house and buy a new 1959 Ford. While he was on the job, Daddy was sending money to the man who was building the house, and by the time he finished the job and came home, the house was almost ready to move into.

It cost $11,000 to build the house in 1959. As it was going up, we were proudly watching the progress. Mama drove by one day, and told Daddy that she thought the house looked too small. She insisted on an additional room, and Daddy agreed. A formal living room was added, and it was obvious that it was an afterthought. We literally had to walk through one of the bedrooms to get to that room, which was filled with fancy white furniture. The room was added simply for prestige.

I was in the sixth grade when we moved into the brick house. This is only the second time in my childhood that I remember Janet being there. Previously, I recall accidentally catching her hair on fire when a hairspray bottle exploded while I was burning trash in a rusted 55-gallon drum. We were playing near it, and I had to put out the fire. That was while the house was being built, and we were living with Mama's sister and her husband in a cabin.

I can't remember actually moving in, but I can remember being happy that we finally had a house. After we moved into the new house, things seemed to start off well. The Atlanta job had provided all the material riches Mama and Daddy had never had. I felt we had made the transition from poverty to the middle class. We were riding high, but somehow, I always felt a little anxiety and uncertainty, even amongst the visible prosperity.

The brick house was home from 1959 to 1962. I remember one day when it snowed, and how much fun it was to be able to stay out of school that day in the new house. I raised a pig there for FFA when I was old enough, and had my 14th birthday party there. I celebrated winning first prize in the 7th grade Science Fair after building an operating incubator for chickens where they could hatch eggs. Several people from my class came to the house to see the project. I had used a light bulb for heat, a wick to add humidity, and a thermometer to make sure the temperature was just right. Then, one day I saw a chicken pecking from inside an egg, and they began hatching one by one. That was an exciting time for a young kid.

When our school gym replaced their basketball goals, I managed to rescue one of the old goals to put up in the woods behind the house. I was so proud of it, I spent hours clearing the woods and cutting limbs off a tree so we could hang it. I recall that day vividly, because I climbed the tree to hang the goal and as I slid down the tree, it scraped up my chest. I even removed stumps and ran electricity up there for lights and a radio. I wouldn't have known it then, but that goal would be my saving grace for several reasons.

It felt like we had all the material possessions in the world, but it was just false prosperity. The chaos would soon begin. Mama caught Daddy running around, and though this was not unusual, it caused a lot of fights. Daddy didn't work during much of this time, so he decided to bootleg on Sundays to make money. Someone sold him beer at wholesale prices, and we'd put it in an old Coca Cola cooler. I would sit in the pump house all day, and people would pull up and buy the beer.

When Daddy was drinking, he would send me to the store in the car, though I was only twelve years old. I even drove to a friend's birthday party when I was fourteen. Her Dad was the Sheriff at the time, and he never said a word about the fact that I was driving. He knew I drove all the time.

I should probably go ahead and tell you that Daddy wrecked every single car he ever owned. Whenever he left the house, he was so drunk that I knew it would only be a matter of time before someone came to the door to let us know he had either wrecked or had been arrested. Or both. One time he wrecked and landed in the water upside down. He was shouting dramatically for someone to come and get him out. The water was only six inches deep, but he was too drunk to realize that. He got another car right after that, then totaled that one within just a few days.

I kept asking Daddy for a car, and one day he gave me a 1959 Ford. He bought a hot motor for it, although I didn't know it at the time. He said, "This is your car, son". I was fourteen at the time, and so proud of that car. I spent so much time putting in the motor and seat covers, and cleaning it up. I used to hide it between trees in the woods above the house because I thought Daddy couldn't get it out, and I knew that if he did, he'd wreck it.

Then one morning around 2am a man knocked on our door. Daddy was gone, so I answered the door. I knew the man, who was a barber at the time. He said, "Listen Gene, my car is down the road a bit. I have liquor on me and I ran out of gas. Can you help?" I said I'd siphon some gas from my car, so I did, and he took off. The next morning, I got up and my car was gone. He had come by to see if Daddy was there. When he found out he wasn't there, he came back later and stole my car.

We ended up carless after all that because Daddy had wrecked everything else. But here's the real kicker. Years later, Mama claimed Daddy had my '59 Ford stolen because I wouldn't let him drive it. Not long before he passed away, I asked Daddy if he had the Ford stolen, and he wouldn't even look at me. He didn't answer. I knew he did it.

After that, the shit really hit the fan. We started getting notices that Daddy owed money because he had borrowed against the house. He borrowed a few thousand dollars to live on, and was not paying it back because he wasn't working. He was just spending. Mama was drunk and Daddy couldn't be found for days at a time. Mama sent me to the grocery store to get things on credit. We had credit at every store in Silver City. Thank goodness, they let me get the groceries.

I'd come home often to find beer all over the kitchen floor where they had been throwing it at each other. Our nice furniture Mama used to be so proud of was tossed around and torn to pieces, and there were holes in the sheetrock. When things got bad like that, as they often did, I would go up into the woods and play basketball. During one of those instances, it was misting rain and ice and I remember the ice just flying off the ball and goal as I shot.

One morning I awoke once again to their cussing and fighting. I heard a shot, and came out of my bedroom to see Mama shooting at Daddy. She continued to shoot as he was going out the door. When he got outside, she shot for a sixth time, but had missed him every time. She was definitely trying to hit him. It was very traumatic for me. My response that day is a complete blank. I know it happened, but I don't know what I did in the moment. I do know that there are still five bullet holes somewhere in that house today.

During another traumatic event, Daddy was driving behind the school bus one afternoon in an old trip car, a 1946 Ford. He had been drinking, and started to go around the bus, and I told him not to do that. A young girl got off the bus and as she was crossing the street, he hit her. Her toboggan flew into the air and landed on our hood, her shoes came off her feet, and her satchel fell to the ground.

He got out of the car and went crazy. He picked her up off the ground, and the next car that came by, he begged them to take her to the hospital. They agreed, and he climbed into the car with her, leaving me behind at the scene. I didn't know whether to move the car or what to do, because I didn't have a license, and there were cops everywhere.

All of these events just piled onto one another, and I was getting so tired of feeling anxious and angry. One night I was so fed up and I told both Mama and Daddy that if I came home one more time to hear them fighting, I'd beat both their asses. And you can probably guess that it didn't have an effect on them at all. Just a few nights later, the fighting happened again.

As I was getting out of my car, I heard them yelling and throwing things. I stormed up to the front door, ready to light into them both, but Daddy had locked the door. I screamed at him through the door, threatening him again. We could see each other through the glass window at the top of the door. He simply put his thumbs in both ears, wagging his fingers like a child. There was an old glass Coke bottle on the porch, and I grabbed it and put it through the window, right at his head.

My finger was almost completely severed. It just fell over onto my palm. We didn't have a car at the time. All we had was a motorcycle. So, me and Mama jumped on the motorcycle for the 30-minute ride to Cumming. Mama would work the gas and I worked the brake. We were covered with blood by the time we arrived at the doctor's office.

The old doctor came into the room, and he was also drunk. He said, "What the fuck did you do to your hand? How did you do that?". I told him that I was running out the door and my hand got hung in the window. He sewed it up, and asked me to hold up my hand when he was done. My finger promptly fell back down again, and he had to sew it all over again. He was trying to sew the ligament back together straight, but instead, he lapped it with the stitch. There's still a lump on that finger today. Daddy didn't go with us that night, and he never asked about it.

CHAPTER 3:
The Day I Started Drinking

Once we moved into the brick house, I thought we had every material possession that we truly needed. However, we couldn't enjoy it for all the chaos. I didn't realize it then, but each chaotic occurrence was forming my future as an addict. Alcohol had become part of the fabric of my life. Every day, every decision, and every dilemma seemed to be connected to drinking.

For Daddy and Mama, being drunk became the norm, and I just couldn't seem to get away from it. Every time Daddy left the driveway, I felt a pang of looming disaster. And that wasn't the only thing I had to worry about, because when Daddy wasn't home, Mama was drunk, too. Sometimes at night from my bedroom, I could hear her dancing with other men in the kitchen. She had locked the doors leading into the living room so I couldn't get in.

It turned my stomach, and not just because it was wrong for a wife and mother to behave that way, but because I knew it would turn into more arguments and more violence once Daddy found out.

Even when they were out partying together, I was bootlegging beer for Daddy. At almost every turn, I was faced with some event that involved alcohol. And when I wasn't involuntarily thrown into the daily activities, I was trying actively to get my mind off of them. I would walk up into the woods to play basketball to escape as much of it as I could, even for a few minutes at a time. I remember wishing with all my might that they could see their mistakes, and realize that we could live a normal life as a family if the drinking just stopped.

At fourteen, I was already an angry child. I felt so much rage, and I didn't know what to do with those feelings. I could never really find relief, and when you can't impact what's happening around you, you have two choices. You can either leave the situation, or embrace the chaos in ways that you feel you *can* control. As a teenage boy, it was pretty obvious to me that I couldn't leave. I had little understanding of how the world worked, and so I just parroted the attitudes and actions that I had seen, somehow believing that I had a modicum of control in the outcome.

The life Daddy and Mama lived was all they really knew, and it became all that I knew by default. At the time, I didn't have any mentors or role models to emulate. It felt like 'me against the world', and that eventually became a self-fulfilling prophecy that would manifest itself in many ways, beginning with the day I started drinking.

That fateful evening that I began my own addictive journey would usher in a new pattern and path for me. It started like any other day. I was actually bootlegging beer from our kitchen, and a friend of mine came by the house to hang out one night. He knew we had Busch Bavarian beer in the fridge, and he wanted one. He wanted me to drink it with him, but I was insistent that I didn't want any part of it. I told him, "I don't want to be like Mama and Daddy."

I was convicted, because I had witnessed and lived in the depths of the drama it had caused for so long. But he persisted, and went to the cupboard and got two coffee cups, and poured the tall beer into the cups. He said, "Here, just drink half of this one", as he pushed the cup toward me. I was growing weary of his attempts, and reasoned with myself that it couldn't really do any harm to have half of one beer.

But that one turned into more, and that night we ended up sharing a total of five beers between us. I was drunk as hell. Another friend stopped by and asked, "Gene, what the hell is wrong with you?" And all I could say was, "I'm drunk". I threw up five times that night, one time for every beer we shared. I was so sick I'll never forget it.

The next day was Sunday, and I always went to shoot basketball at the gym on Sundays. I hitchhiked to the gym because Daddy had wrecked all the cars. I walked for a while until someone picked me up, and every single step was so painful. I was pushing hard against the pain caused in one short evening. I even said out loud, "I'm so sick, I can't stand it. I'll never drink again."

Mama and Daddy even knew I was drunk when they came home. They heard me retching in the bathroom each time I got up. They never said a thing to me about it. There was no ridicule, but there were no questions, help or understanding, either.

The next weekend, I got drunk again. I came home drunk, and that's the night when I put the Coke bottle through the door, aiming for Daddy. Thinking back to that moment, I wonder now what would have happened if I hadn't injured myself and been forced to seek medical help. Could I have actually done irreversible harm to them both? It's a question that has haunted me for years, and one for which I have no clear answer. I'd like to think I would have stopped short of killing them both, but in the most truthful part of my soul, I know that in that moment, all I felt was the rage, and I just wanted it all to end.

My drinking continued. I didn't drink every day, especially during basketball season, because it was the one thing in my life that provided a sense of confidence and pride. But I made plenty of bad decisions in between. I became well known among my friends as someone who could get beer anywhere. I knew the location of every bootlegger along every road leading outside of Dawsonville. As Glenn Odom's son, I could get beer from all of them with no questions asked.

With that freedom came other freedoms, like fast and reckless driving. I straight-wired a '57 Chevy that

Daddy had bought, and when he wasn't home, my friend and I would drag race with that car and my '59 Ford. In some ways, it was a freedom that I felt was owed to me because of the life I was forced to live. I embraced those events with reckless abandon, but they ended up ironically just wrecking more of my life.

In fact, the first car I wrecked was a 1957 Mercury that I had driven to school a few times. I had been practicing turning into my driveway while hitting the gas hard, attempting to go up the driveway sideways. I had created what I thought was the perfect system, and looking back, I still believe it was pretty damn good. I could take the turn into the driveway doing 40 or 50 miles per hour, and fishtail into my spot. *Sideways left, sideways right, sideways left, then right into the spot.*

I was so determined and intense about this one thing that I took the fenders off so I could see which way I needed to turn the wheels to make it happen flawlessly. One day while I was driving home from school with my friend, Jimmy Tatum, I decided to show him what I could do. As I was attempting this perfect system once again, this time I hit a tree and busted the radiator, busted a tire, and destroyed the fender and hood. The car was totaled, and Tatum suffered injuries he remembers to this day.

Next up was a 1956 Buick Century, which I ran into a lake. That area of the lake was like a marsh, and the

Buick sank into it, with mud reaching halfway up the doors. I was trying to get out, and luckily, I finally got the windows to open. It didn't hurt the car that badly, but it was stuck and I had to walk back home. When Mama got home, I told her what I'd done and she got some people we knew to pull it out. I cleaned it for two days trying to get the mud out.

There wasn't a scratch anywhere except the rear hubcaps. In trying desperately to drive it out of the lake, the turn of the rear wheels had made scratches on the hubcaps that looked like perfect rings. I thought Daddy wouldn't notice it, and when he came back from being on the road, the first thing he said was, "What the hell happened to those hubcaps?" I told him I had no idea. Mama didn't say a thing, either. Daddy just said, "By god, that's the strangest thing I've ever seen".

I was actually not drinking during either of those accidents. I do realize in hindsight, though, that the drinking lifestyle was definitely to blame for this type of behavior. I was doing everything I could to drown out the pain. And when I acted like a big shot, it not only helped me escape a few moments at a time, it seemed to help me gain more confidence in myself back then. Of course, I know now that it wasn't really confidence that I was gaining. It was more chaos.

When I went out on Friday nights with the boys, I was one of youngest of the group, and I drove frequently because most of them didn't know how. I got the beer because they couldn't. It gained me attention, and that was what I was desperately seeking. I liked the attention. It felt good to me, because I got a little relief from all the drama.

When I got drunk, the problems seemed farther away. It was the first time I experienced escaping, and it felt good. Back then I thought I was just having fun. But I was really fighting pain. When you go into the house wanting to kill your Daddy, that's pain.

One of the most destructive things that comes from attempting to escape pain with alcohol or drugs is that it makes you selfish. You depend only on yourself, mostly because you live in a world where you don't have anyone else to depend on. It was a protective mode I put myself in many times, and it affected all of my relationships. It's a vicious cycle that just repeats itself, over and over.

I feel as though I've taken care of Gene my whole life. I took care of my family as much as I could, but when I got on drugs, it was all about Gene. I didn't know that then, but I do now. Looking back through all those years of addiction, I was just repeating the actions and behaviors of a fourteen year old boy. I didn't want any pain, and I did what I felt I needed to do to compensate. When you're drinking or on drugs, nothing bothers you. You don't feel the pain. And just when you think you've overcome the addiction, something can happen that brings all that pain back to the surface. And then you fall again.

CHAPTER 4:
Then Daddy Went to Prison

Even while Daddy was working on the big job at Moreland Avenue that had brought in enough money to pay for the house, he had at least two legal cases pending. One of the charges was for manufacturing non-tax paid whiskey. Another was a conspiracy charge. So, throughout all the time we lived in the brick house, he was fully aware that his time would come to pay the piper. I'm certain that realization elevated his drinking even more.

I had no idea about those cases or potential sentencing until shortly before his downfall. And although times were turbulent, strangely, no one in the family ever talked about it, or the fact that he could possibly go to prison. It's hard to believe that everyone kept things so quiet, but that was also part of the moonshiner's code. In fact, I only became aware of the impending trouble when I overheard Mama's conversations with family members.

I remember the hanging feeling of doom and uncertainty, and I was afraid to broach the subject with Daddy because it was so sensitive. I think we were all individually trying to pretend the situation didn't exist. But I could see everything falling apart. The cold chill of what was to come lingered like a stark and unforgiving winter. I constantly worried and wondered what would happen next.

By this time, we were down to one car again. I was in my Freshman year of high school then. This was the car that I parked in the woods, thinking it might be too much trouble for Daddy to get it out, and it might actually be safe there.

He had not only wrecked all of his own cars, but he had caused the demise of two others he had borrowed. His brother-in-law let him borrow a car, and he had driven it through the woods until it was ruined with scratches. Then, he borrowed a car from a friend. When he pulled into the driveway in that second borrowed car, I could tell Mama was extremely angry. He always managed to find a car, but never cared whether she had anything to drive.

The next day I was headed to school, and I saw the car Daddy had just borrowed, sitting on the side of the road. The windows looked black, like they had been tinted. I thought that was very strange, but by this time, strange was normal. When I got home that day, I found out that Mama had driven it away from the house and set it on fire.

Things were definitely getting worse. There was no money coming in, and groceries were scarce. Daddy was partying his ass off, as though it was his last hoorah. And as destiny would prove, it certainly would be. He didn't have a job, and the debt was piling up. We had been extended credit from what seemed like every place in town. We owed a Phillips 66 station for gas. We owed two garages for keeping the cars maintained. We owed four different grocery stores. We ran up grocery bills to the tune of $200 or $300 per location, which was a lot of money in those days. That wasn't unusual for moonshiners, though. Most of them were known for keeping their word and paying their debts. After all, if a man didn't pay his debts, word got around really fast, and he would lose business and the ability to carry credit anywhere. And since the moonshine business was feast or famine, you needed those lifelines. Daddy had always kept his word where his creditors were concerned, so they allowed the debt to continue to climb.

As the debt piled up, so did the bad decisions. There was one car accident after another, violent arguments, shattered glass, and broken promises. And in true Glenn Odom form, one more dramatic incident would be his undoing, bringing forth his destiny even sooner.

Daddy left home drunk again, this time in my car. Turns out, it wasn't safe after all. In fact, he wasn't just drunk, either. He was soused. I had that gut feeling again, and said to myself, "He will have a wreck. Somebody's gonna knock on the door and we'll find out he's either in jail or dead."

He made it as far as the green bridge on Hwy 53, headed toward Gainesville. He came down the hill toward the bridge running 110 miles per hour, quickly approaching a '49 Chevrolet right in front of him. He came down the hill so fast that he didn't even notice the car until the last minute. He swung left to pass the car, and just as he was passing, another truck was approaching from the opposite direction.

In a flash, he was forced to squeeze between the two cars, and the collision shaved off both sides of his car as he passed between them. It happened so fast that the man driving one of the other vehicles said he didn't even know he had been hit until his kids began complaining about water coming in through the hole that was torn in the rear door of the car. There was water on the roadway from a previous rain, and the tires were slinging the water up into the back seat.

Daddy continued to speed beyond the two vehicles he had hit for another half mile or so, until guilt came over him. It was likely the same guilt I witnessed when he hit the little girl who was getting off the bus. And it's the same trait that, despite his obstinacy and violent tendencies, made me have compassion for him. He knew he had to go back to see if he had hurt anyone. As he headed back toward the scene of the accident, he was forced to stick his head out the driver's window in order to see because his hood had been forced upward, blocking his view.

Witnesses say he was still running wide open when he returned. They could hear him coming down the road because the accident had also knocked off his muffler. The other drivers and their passengers were standing on the roadside for safety, and thank goodness, because Daddy was still driving so recklessly that he actually rear-ended the same truck he had hit before, and finally came to a stop.

There were three adults and five kids in the accident that day, and God was certainly looking after them all. No one was hurt except for Daddy, who had a cut on his chin that later required stitches. Furthermore, I'm not sure exactly how the miracle continued, but Daddy actually left the scene with a friend before the law arrived. Ironically, both cars he hit were from Dawson County.

I was at home this whole time, pacing the floors back and forth to the kitchen window, hoping he would return safely. I was worried to death. All of a sudden, a car pulled up, and he got out. I still don't know who brought him home, but by the time he reached the kitchen door, there were cop cars everywhere. There were about seven car loads of state patrol right on his heels. It reminded me of the movie, *Sugarland Express.*

They flew into the driveway, parking haphazardly, and rushed the front door. They were pissed. They burst in without knocking, and they didn't have a search warrant. They didn't say anything to me, and I said nothing to them. I figure they knew his days were numbered, too, so they just grabbed his ass and took him in. That night, they locked him up, and a few hours later, someone made his bond. After he was let out, he went to the hospital, where they put several stitches in his chin. That was near the end of his free days.

A few days after the accident, I asked someone to take me to the garage where my car had been towed. When I pulled in to see it, I just said out loud, "Oh my God." The car was so destroyed, I couldn't believe what I was seeing. Both sides of the vehicle were ripped off. The front of the car had been pushed back so far that the steering column was sticking up through the roof. The hood was up, mirrors were ripped off, and every piece of glass was broken. There was not one piece of anything on that car that was worth keeping. And there on the front seat sat a pint of white liquor, which had probably been wedged between the seats and later moved. I never saw my car again.

Shortly after this occurrence, Daddy was offered a plea deal. They told him they would clear all pending cases if he would agree to build four years in prison. I never knew the details of what was at stake or why he agreed, but he made the deal.

As would become the pattern in some of the more life-altering moments, I don't remember the details of the day Daddy actually left for prison. I vaguely remember riding with someone to take him to the federal building in Gainesville, and watching him walk into the building carrying a small bag of clothes. The first several months of his sentence would be at the penitentiary in Tallahassee, Florida. In those days, they started inmates out in a location farther from home. I was told that they did this to encourage good behavior, because if the prisoners did well for a few months, they would likely transfer them closer to home. It was supposedly their way of controlling the chaos a little. After Tallahassee, he would be moved to Atlanta, where he would build the remainder of his four year sentence.

Right after he was moved to Atlanta, we visited him one Sunday. As soon as we walked inside the prison, I had a sobering, eerie feeling. I instantly knew it was a place I could never be. I would never belong there. But I didn't exactly envy being on the outside, either. I was now the man of the house, and we were on the verge of losing everything. It was a responsibility I didn't seek or want, and I felt I could only rely on what I had witnessed in my fourteen years so far. That was the liquor business.

I remembered how Daddy had brought home all that money in just a few months, and how it had changed everything almost overnight. It seemed to me that the only way out of this was to continue what Daddy and Mama had started, and do my best to bail us out. So, I began a brief conversation that would shape me in more ways than my innocent young mind could conceive as the words so effortlessly flowed from my mouth.

I said, "Daddy, if I dug out from under the house and put a still under there, reckon we could save the house?" Inwardly, I was thinking we could get someone he knew to build the still. I could help to run it, and we'd find someone else to sell the liquor. Just like they had done for years. In my simple mind, it was a simple solution. And it was a last ditch effort.

He never laughed or scoffed at my idea. He answered me just like I was asking for directions to the nearest Coke machine. He said, "Son, you can try it, but I don't think that will work." I just stared stoically ahead and replied, "I'm gonna try it."

CHAPTER 5:
Digging the Hole

After I returned from visiting Daddy at the prison, I was energized. You know the feeling you get when you believe you've figured out a solution to a massive problem? It's a relief, and even though you know in your heart that it's a fantastic long shot, it gives you temporary reprieve from all the turmoil.

When we think back on decisions from our past, those moments in the crosshairs and crossroads of life, the outcome is so clear. But in the moment, you're full of hope. You turn a blind eye to the details and focus on the desired outcome. That's an incredible trait in most cases, but a foolish one in circumstances such as these. I *had* to know it wouldn't work.

I obviously didn't know much as a young teenage boy, but I did know for damn certain that I didn't want to be poor again. I didn't want to live in a house with eight people. And I didn't want to lose the only structure that we had been able to call home. Not necessarily because it felt warm and inviting, but because it was ours.

Amid all the confusion was a deep seeded reaction that only a young child can justify. I felt sorry for Daddy. Despite everything he had done, and not done. Despite his reckless attitude and selfish actions. Despite all the things I would have a hard time forgiving for years to come. He had worked so hard to provide the home, the furniture, and the cars. And it was clear to me that Mama wasn't doing her part. She wouldn't work, and she only participated in the liquor business when she had no choice. It had all culminated in this moment, where I was standing in the yard alone, hoping to be the hero.

I had a Radio Flyer wagon and a toy shovel made out of metal. It was small, but it would be sturdy enough to do the job. At the end of the house where we had built the new room, there was an entrance to a crawl space that led to the furnace, which was positioned near the middle of the house. It was about 2.5 feet high, so you could crawl to the furnace if you needed to work on it. I imagined if I could just dig and make that hole deep enough to hold a still, I might be able to sell enough liquor to hang onto the house until Daddy got out of prison.

My young survivalist mentality set in and I began to dig with the energy and fervor of a young soldier during his first week at boot camp. I can't remember the exact time of year, but it must have been springtime, because I don't remember being cold. I didn't have a light, so I dug mostly during daylight. I just had a radio to keep me company.

When I was under the house, it was just me. Daddy had taught me to be so secretive about anything regarding moonshine. Mama was the only one who knew what I was doing at the time, and she never said a word to me about digging the hole. I think she was just glad to have me out of the house so she could do whatever she wanted without having me in the way. And honestly, at first it was peaceful because there was no more screaming and fighting. It was like one burden had been lifted, but another had landed.

I dug for days. I had scooped thousands of shovelfuls of dirt into my wagon, and at one point, the wagon became so heavy and the hole was so deep that I couldn't get it out. I had dug chest-deep. I grabbed two wooden planks from the yard and positioned them like a ramp leading out of the hole, and then I began to drag each load up the planks. The yard was full of holes here and there, and uneven, so I took each load of dirt and strategically dumped it into the yard in an attempt to make the ground more level.

I can still smell that damp, earthy smell sometimes, and it subconsciously and instantly brings me right back to that hole, and that feeling of desperation.

Looking back, I would have expected Mama to intervene, to put me out of my misery. I would have expected her to say, "Son, I know you have good intentions, but you're wasting your time. You know that will never work." But all she did was ignore it.

Although I had dug so much, I don't remember any physical pain. But I do recall the pain of feeling alone. As much as I had toiled and despite my virtuous intentions, it would never work. Reality had hit me like a ton of bricks. It's an age old saying, but in my case, it was ironic because that's exactly what the house above me had become. Nothing more than a ton of bricks, weighing heavily on my ailing shoulders and fragile soul.

So, on a seemingly random day, in dark and despair, I laid down the small shovel and crawled up out of the hole. My spirit had finally broken.

I don't know what I did or where I went the day I laid the shovel down. I just knew I was tired. I gave up. I saw how long I'd been digging, and how little I'd accomplished. Yes, the hole was sizable, but that was only a small part of the solution. Who would help me build the still? Who would make the liquor? Who would sell it? And who would deliver it? And even if I knew those answers, who could I really trust?

The house was gone, and I might as well embrace that truth. In the beginning, I felt heroic. I just knew I could save the home and put food back on the table. I wanted to provide for my Mama, and I wanted Daddy to be proud of me when he returned home. But as the hole got larger, I realized the enormity of my circumstances.

I learned a critical lesson that day. I was alone in this world. This awareness had cracked the shell of a rebellious nature that would follow me like an unrelenting shadow. It would give me strength, but it would also cause such uncertainty deep in my soul that it would rear its head in literally every situation and relationship from that point forward.

Almost 50 years later, I noticed that the old brick house was for sale. I pulled into the driveway one afternoon and spoke to the owner. I told him that I used to live there, and a little about my childhood. I mentioned the hole that I had dug so many years earlier, and asked if I could see it. As we walked through the yard toward the end of the house, a familiar wave of dread washed over me.

I could feel it in the pit of my stomach, and I started to become a little nauseous. As I stood near the entryway of the hole, peering down into my past, I remember being so surprised at what I had done all those years ago. The hole was almost large enough to fit a Volkswagen Beetle inside. I choked back the tears as I remembered so vividly the feeling of that tiny metal shovel in my hand.

As I leaned in closer, I could see just one remnant of those days, covered in the red dust of half a century, but still visible, as though it was waiting for this crowning moment of awareness. There was one beer can still in the hole.

CHAPTER 6:
Wealth Just Walked Away

I can only recall a few times when I was growing up that everything was quiet and peaceful at home. Those moments were in the mornings, and I could hear Mama and Daddy in bed talking. They were smoking cigarettes and drinking coffee, and they were sober. I ran in there and jumped in bed with them to join the conversation. In those few precious moments, we felt like a family, and even though I was young, I knew that was what wealth was really all about. I didn't need the brick house, the fancy furniture, or all the fast cars. And as it turns out, I ended up having none of those things.

The bills had piled up, from groceries to garages to personal loans. One of Daddy's friends had even loaned him a few thousand dollars to help us get by, and he was demanding repayment. He could see the writing on the wall. Mama knew she wouldn't have anything once Daddy went to prison. Not even the house that she loved so much, or the spotless white furniture from the room no one ever sat in. Everything they had built together was crumbling like a house of cards.

It seemed like each day when I got home from school, something else was missing from the house. From pieces of furniture to the stereo, it was disappearing one small piece at a time. Mama was trading these items for liquor. She didn't have a job, and was drunk most of the time. Daddy was in prison, and I was struggling to figure out what I could do to help beyond the hole digging project I had just abandoned. Truth be told, I didn't want to deal with any of it, and yet I carried the weight of it even in my sleep. I was exhausted from worry, and I had no one in my life to lead me in the right direction.

Daddy would occasionally write from prison, and all of his letters started with the same greeting. "How are y'all? Fine, I hope." I wondered how he could inject such calmness into those letters, as though he's conversing about the weather. Life was falling apart, and he was sheltered from the result of his decisions, albeit behind bars.

I couldn't help feeling sorry for all of us, myself included. This was the first time we had our own home. In this home, I had learned to lean on basketball as an escape, and it quickly became my first love. It was where I had my 14th birthday party, and where my eighth grade basketball coach, Ford Phillips, would drop me off after practice.

I'll never forget the day he came into the house and told Mama that I had a pretty good chance of playing on the Varsity team in the upcoming school year. To be on the Varsity team as a Freshman was a big deal, and I longed for that spot. I was on cloud nine that day. It was not only a great source of accomplishment and pride for me, but I desperately wanted Mama and Daddy to be proud of me, too. Despite the turmoil, it had been the only home I had known, and the source of some impressionable memories.

After I had stopped digging the hole underneath the house, there was tension in the air, always. I had gotten so accustomed to the drama and the stress, that I began to block things out. It's truly the only explanation I have for not remembering some of the most pivotal points of those days.

I don't remember the events that occurred the day the house sold, but I do recall the day the notice appeared on the door. The house would be put up for auction. Panic set in for Mama, and she went to Gainesville to speak with several real estate companies, trying to find a solution so we could keep the house. Her efforts were fruitless, and the shift began.

During one of our trips to visit Daddy in prison, he had given me clear instructions that I was to carry out as soon as the house was sold. He said, "Son, the first thing you have to do is pay everybody we owe. Then, whatever is left, make it go as far as you can."

The next thing I recall is the day a truck showed up to load up all of our furniture and take it away. I was just standing there frozen in the driveway, watching it all happen like it was someone else's life. They took the furniture to a storage facility in Gainesville, where it remained for four years while Daddy was in prison. Shortly after he was released from prison, he went to the storage building to see what it would take to get the furniture out. He found the belongings covered in mold and mildew, barely salvageable. The strange thing is, he didn't have the money to get it out even if it was worth keeping.

I often wondered what would make a man back track like that, knowing he probably wouldn't be able to get that furniture back. Was he lamenting the past? Did he go there so it would serve as a reminder for the future? Why would someone choose to revisit the pain of the past? It's ironic how I asked myself that question about the furniture, but not about the everyday choices they made that got us to that point. Why indeed would a man revisit a painful past?

The house was auctioned off by Waldrip Realty out of Gainesville for $14,000. I don't recall the day of the auction. I'm not even sure where I was when the house sold, but I'll never forget hearing the news of who had purchased it. Ford Phillips, my basketball coach, had actually purchased the home for his son and daughter in law. Ford had brought me home after practice many evenings, dropping me off in the same driveway that would now belong to his family.

In a normal situation, you'd think I would have been bitter about that, or at least questioned the outcome. Instead, I actually felt a little relieved. At least someone I cared about and respected would benefit from all the bad decisions we had made. That feeling struck me as a little odd, because I think it was the first time I realized that I had reached a level of maturity that was already well beyond the capabilities of my parents. It was indeed a strange feeling.

So, here we were without a home. We had no car of our own, and even the borrowed cars had either been destroyed or returned. All I had was the red motorcycle that me and Mama had driven to the doctor's office when I cut my hand on the front door glass. If uncertainty had plagued our family before, this was a whole new level.

All I could focus on was the instructions from Daddy. "The first thing you have to do is pay everybody we owe. Then, whatever is left, make it go as far as you can." Mama gave me the money a bit at a time so I could get everyone paid. I guess she put that responsibility on my shoulders because she couldn't bear to face the people we owed, and she also didn't want to deal with the business end of things due to her lack of education. This was a woman who had ordered an additional room built onto our home simply because she didn't think it looked big enough from the road. And now, most of what was left of our little estate would be returned to our creditors.

I was aware of every creditor, and exactly how much we owed each one. After all, I was the one they sent to the grocery stores and garages. Mama doled out the amounts of money one at a time for each creditor, and I had to pay them one by one. After the last person was paid, there was two thousand dollars left over. I brought every penny home to Mama and handed it to her.

That same night, me and Janet ended up at Aunt Ethel's house. Ethel was Dad's sister, and the strength and matriarch of the family. Mama told us she'd see us later on. A night went by, then another. Days, then weeks. We didn't see Mama again for a year. We didn't even know where she was. No phone calls, no visits, no birthday cards, nothing.

When you view life through a lens of material wealth, you begin to take for granted the more meaningful things. I never imagined my Daddy would end up in prison. And I certainly didn't imagine my Mama would leave us of her own accord for an entire year.

While this turning point may seem to be one of the most harrowing yet, the four years that followed would actually do more to grow my independence and determination than anything I had experienced thus far. Wealth (as I knew it) may have walked away, and my spirit may have been broken again, but it was still there. And it was about to grow wings.

CHAPTER 7:
New Surroundings for Survival

The good years go by fast. I was at my Aunt Ethel's from 1962 to 1966. Even though we only occupied three rooms in the house, we made it work, and Ethel made it feel like home. There was only one bedroom with two double beds. Janet and Ethel slept in one bed, and Ronald, Ethel's son, slept in the other. Harold, Ethel's invalid brother, slept on a twin bed in the living room. And I slept on the couch during all four years.

Ethel was my Dad's sister, and one of ten siblings. Their mom passed away from pneumonia when Ethel was just a teenager, leaving her and her sister, Ailene, to take care of the younger children. Their twin brothers, Edgar and George, were only six months old at the time of their mother's death. Ethel immediately took George under her wing, while Ailene cared for Edgar. So, from a very early age, she was responsible for the daily care of an infant and had multiple mouths to feed. She and her sisters cooked for the whole family while the older boys worked in the fields.

Ethel's role as caretaker became the norm throughout her lifetime, as she cared for her son, her brother, and several children who were lucky enough to spend time in her home. When I lived with Ethel, we shared the home with an elderly lady named Bell, who lived in the two other rooms of the house, which consisted of a bedroom and small kitchen. Ethel made most of the meals for her and helped to look after her in exchange for lower rent.

Bell was an incredibly sweet woman who kept to herself most of the time. She rarely traveled, except to church. I can remember the 1955 Ford she drove to Harmony Baptist Church, just down the road. Her daughter, Grace, lived across the street with her husband, Hoyt 'Doc' Robertson. And her son, Alton, and his family lived in Gainesville. On Sundays, her family would often visit and we'd all sit on the big wraparound porch together overlooking the four-way stop and Doc's gas station and store across the street.

Though we were crammed into a tight space, it was the most peaceful time I'd experienced so far in my life. I didn't have to listen to the bullshit or hear the fighting. We always had something to eat, which was better than I had been getting at home. Mama had made grits for breakfast almost every morning, and the only choice I had was, "Do you want your grits with or without salt?

I felt grateful because Ethel was known throughout the entire county for her southern cooking. We regularly had fried chicken, green beans, mashed potatoes, potato salad, macaroni and cheese, and sweet tea. She fed us well on her meager salary. I remember many nights after basketball games, I'd come home to a huge stack of warm homemade peanut butter cookies sitting on the kitchen table. Those are fond memories, and I felt safe during those four years.

Ethel's home was on the corner of Hwy 53 and Lumpkin Campground Road, a busy area of our small town. Doc's store was on the opposite side of the street, and there were steps built into the hill leading down from Ethel's house to the store. The home was an older Victorian style home, with pretty much no insulation. In fact, you could see daylight through some of the wood slats in the walls. We had a gas heater in the living room as our only source of heat. In the spring and summer, we left the windows open at night and used box fans to cool the house.

When the windows were open, I could hear cars stopping at Doc's store, and people getting out to get a drink from the Coke machine. You could clearly hear their conversations, many of them cursing, which made me laugh and shake my head. I still recall the familiar sound of the drink bottles as they dropped to the bottom of the machine and the loud chirping of crickets on a summer night.

Ethel's son, Ronald, had a speech impediment that plagued him until the day he passed away. He lived with her his entire life. I mostly remember how he loved to eat, and when Ethel would make a large pot of pinto beans, his plate would be piled so high that I couldn't imagine eating that much at one time. And he loved hot peppers, and frequently tried to entice kids to try them, laughing heartily when they made a bitter face. He loved to hunt and fish with a good friend of his, and would spend time with him, though infrequently. He was also a huge John Wayne fan.

Ronald would occasionally help Doc Robertson bale hay, or help Ethel in the garden, but he only held an official job once in his life. He worked at the rubber plant across the street and up the hill, but only for a few months. As soon as he earned enough money to buy a color TV, a VCR, and some John Wayne movies, he quit his job and never returned to work. He and Ethel had a good dynamic, though. She was always kind and understanding toward him, and he respected her as a mother.

Her brother, Harold, was in a wheelchair most of his life. He was stricken with infantile paralysis as a child, and during his late teens and early twenties, it manifested to the point that he could no longer walk. He was often seen hitch hiking to Dawsonville, and many folks back then remember seeing him fall by the roadside as he was attempting to hitch a ride. That was during the final days before he was confined to a wheelchair. He was the most gentle soul, and happy all the time. I never witnessed him in a bad mood, and he always treated me with kindness.

One day I was inside the house and I heard Harold yelling, followed by a loud crashing noise that sounded like a car accident. He was trying to roll his wheelchair from the porch back into the house and lost control of the brake. He rolled off the steep concrete front porch steps and down into the yard in his wheelchair. The front porch was tilted downward toward the yard, which no doubt helped to give him more momentum. When I reached him, the wheels were still spinning so fast they made a whirring sound. I don't see how he survived it, but it didn't even hurt him. He was known for being very tough.

He was completely dependent on Ethel, who fed him, bathed him and made all of his meals. Whenever she went somewhere, Harold would often accompany her. I remember him sitting at the end of the kitchen table to eat all of his meals from his signature brown dinner plate. The edges of the plate were slightly upturned, making it easier for him to feed himself without scooping his food off onto the table.

For many years, Ethel got up at 4:30 every morning to prepare for work at a chicken processing plant in Gainesville. She got Harold out of bed and changed him, then she cooked breakfast for all of us and made sure we had lunch, too. She caught a ride to work with someone every morning because she didn't have a car.

Harold was two years younger than Ethel, and lived with her until she could no longer physically care for him. He lived the rest of his days completely content in a nursing home in Dahlonega, and Ethel visited him religiously at least once a week.

I knew she was sacrificing for us, even through the eyes of a child at the time. But looking back now at everything she was balancing, I'm in complete awe of her strength and determination. Perhaps most astonishing, I never heard her complain, not even once.

I can recall so many fond memories from my years at Ethel's house. But the strangest thing is that I barely remember my sister, Janet, in my youth. The only moments I remember with any regularity were seeing her in bed with Ethel on Saturday mornings. She rode the school bus with me, but I honestly can't remember any association with her. I guess I was so consumed with taking care of myself. It was almost as though she wasn't there, but she *was* there, every day.

Janet was a quiet child, and I know she had to feel a lot of the same pain and stress that I felt. She'd been through all that misery, too. Later in life, of course, we spent some time together, but we never mentioned our childhood. There was an unspoken understanding between us, but never a concrete bond.

Although I was focused on school and sports, and I was in a safe place, my painful past began to surface. Sometimes it was displayed through normal teenage boy behavior, and other times it was deeper, and more telling.

I was out with several friends one night, and we had been drinking heavily. We decided it would be funny to steal hubcaps from a few cars in Gainesville, which was almost as common back then as rolling yards with toilet paper is today. We didn't think of it as stealing; we simply thought of it as mischievous. That is, until we got caught. It was a traumatic event. We were booked at the police department, an experience that still brings a twinge of guilt even today. The first thing that ran through my mind was...Herbert Robinson.

I was devastated and humiliated. I felt about two inches high. I was walking down the hallway at school just a couple of days after we got caught, hanging my head in shame, just praying he hadn't heard about it. But of course, he had, and he addressed it the first thing Monday morning with several of us in his office. He said, "I heard some of my boys got in trouble over the weekend." Immediately, I raised my hand, willing to accept the consequences.

Later, he came up to me and put his arm around my neck. He said, "Listen son, what you did was wrong. But you made a mistake, and you've learned from it. I don't want to see you walking up and down this hallway hanging your head again." From that day forward, it didn't bother me again. I immediately straightened up, and began to focus on the future. It was such a pivotal moment for me, because it taught me that shame should never define you.

As the months and years went by, I lived as normal a life as possible, especially compared to life before arriving at Ethel's. I cut the grass on Saturdays. And I put up a basketball goal about twenty yards from the house, which is where I spent a lot of time. Morris Martin, a great friend of mine, came over and helped me build a shed for my motorcycle. We built it with some boards from an old house and it had a door on each end so you could drive straight in one side and out the other without having to back the motorcycle out.

One of my favorite stories about Ethel happened when she came home from work one day and announced that she was going to buy a car. She looked me in the eye and boldly proclaimed, "I'm gonna buy a car and you're gonna teach me how to drive." She was 52 years old and had never been behind the wheel of a car.

A few days later, her brother, George, helped her find a box-shaped Chevrolet Malibu. It was blue, which was her favorite color, and a six-cylinder automatic. I climbed into the car with her, prepared to teach her as best I could. She was fearless. She actually scared the hell out of me, and as fearless as I was myself, her driving must have been pretty frightening. But she learned to drive, and it gave her even more independence, which made me proud to be a part of it.

I'm sure Ethel was struggling to keep food on the table for all of us. I tried to be respectful of that, and I don't remember asking Ethel for any money until right before my high school graduation. I had been giving her money to put away for a cap and gown, but when it came time to pay for it, I didn't have quite enough, so she gave me the rest.

Our situation was known by others in the family, who occasionally offered a hand. For instance, I approached my Uncle Edgar when I was in the 10th grade about buying a car from him. He had a 1957 Ford, a custom 300 straight shift in two tone green, with air conditioning. He originally bought it for his son, Stevie, and was planning to give it to him in a few years when he turned 16, so he told me he just couldn't sell it at the time.

Then, during my senior year, Edgar came to me and asked me if I was still interested in the car. I told him yes, but that I didn't have any money. He said, "Come on up here and get it, and pay me when you can." All I had was a motorcycle at the time, and this was a dream come true. One of the proudest days of my life was when I paid him back for the car.

I thought Mama would come back after a little while, but as the weeks dragged on, it became apparent that she wasn't. I can remember being pissed because of the two thousand dollars she'd taken with her. It was the last money we had, and she didn't offer Ethel a nickel when she left.

After everything Ethel was providing for us, I couldn't believe she didn't at least leave a thousand dollars to help us out. But whenever I expressed my anger and said something negative toward Mama, Ethel would put a firm stop to it by saying, "That's your Mama, and don't you talk about her like that."

I was so angry at Mama, though, I had sworn I'd never speak to her again. A year later, she showed up at Ethel's, but I didn't see her that day. Truth be told, I'm not sure if I was home and refused to see her, or if I was gone when she stopped in. But I'm told that she did bring a thousand dollars to give to Ethel. Her visit lasted only a few minutes and she was gone again. She told Ethel she had been working at a nursing home in Tennessee. Although that may have been true for a short time, I did hear later that she had just been a few miles up the road most of that time, living with another man.

She missed all of my high school years. She didn't attend any of my basketball games or even my graduation. Mama never thought much about school, honestly, since she had never attended herself. I didn't see her again until I was married.

I remained angry and bitter about these things for many years until I realized that Mama and Daddy were simply acting upon and reacting to their own experiences. They were just living life to the length of their own understanding.

As I recall those four years at Ethel's house, I realize it was the gateway to my survival. Though I had been tossed involuntarily into new surroundings, it was the first time I felt peace and unconditional love. And if everyone could experience that for even a small amount of time, the length of their understanding would grow well beyond the boundaries of survival.

HONORING AUNT ETHEL

I felt it important to honor the woman who opened her home and heart to me throughout my life. It was without judgment, and most notably, without complaint, that she took me in during a formative time in my youth. I thought this eulogy (written and delivered by Tonya) at Aunt Ethel's funeral would be the perfect way to extend my love and respect for what she brought to me, and meant to me. It's yet another testament to her worth and the impact she had on every life she touched.

Ethel Mae Odum
October 18, 1918 – February 21, 2019
Eulogy delivered at Bearden Funeral Home in Dawsonville, Georgia

To write this speech has taken what feels like a lifetime, and I consider it one of the most important I will ever deliver. I feel an obligation, a calling, to honor the actions of a woman whose *full* journey I will never know. I can only testify to the humility she breathed into mine.

I can share with you how I watched her care for her brother, Harold, who was in a wheelchair most of his life. How she always smiled when she spoke of him, and never once uttered a complaint when she made his breakfast *and lunch* before 6am each day, and returned home after standing on her feet all day at a chicken processing plant, to make his dinner, bathe him, and put him to bed. I remember his heavy, brown dinner plate with the edge slightly upturned, which made it easier for him to feed himself, and every meal was served in it as he occupied the head of the table.

I can share with you how brave she seemed, though her eyes were brimming with tears, the day we drove him to a nursing home together. I was twelve years old. She said I cried the entire way there and back. And I remember vividly how she was insistent that if a nursing home was good enough for Harold, it would certainly be good enough for her one day. She didn't want to be a burden to anyone, though she had carried the burdens of so many without a second thought.

I can share how she taught me how to cook my first fried egg in an iron skillet, while balancing on a wobbly step stool beside her. How she made snow cream for me every time it snowed. She insisted that I scoop the snow off her car because it wouldn't be as dirty as the snow on the ground.

I can share with you how she taught me to crochet and delighted at every mangled potholder or flower I attempted, as though I was a young, budding Picasso. And how she couldn't wait to hear me sing and play my guitar every Saturday night while she was fixing Bell's hair (Bell was the sweet lady who was her roommate for many years, and who first introduced me to church). I remember the sounds of popcorn popping in a worn-out pan that had certainly seen better days.

I remember all the times she pointed from inside her screen door to show me blue jays resting on the clothesline. She spoke in a whisper, though they were fifty yards away, because she didn't want to frighten them. They were her favorite bird, and blue was her favorite color.

I remember how dedicated she was to her son, Ronald. How he completed her life. How she answered his every need until he left this earth too soon, with her sitting, worn and weary, by his bedside.

I recall her rolling laughter when I insisted on eating mustard greens plucked straight from the garden or homemade sauerkraut straight from the mason jar. And especially when Ronald cracked open the hot peppers and challenged me, in hopes that I would react dramatically upon the first taste. Which, of course, I did.

And I remember the Saturday afternoons when she mysteriously showed up to rescue me from picking up sticks and pine cones and raking pine needles from the yard so she could whisk me away for another laid back weekend adventure. Watching her old Nova pull into the driveway felt like the part in a James Bond movie when he appears to rescue a damsel in distress. Only it was me, being rescued from a rake.

I can share with you how I learned to drive in that same Nova. My driving never once seemed to frighten her. Either that, or she was very good at hiding it. I can still smell the inside of that car, and I can still feel the radio buttons, the kind you pushed in, which always seemed to land on gospel or country music. Back then, I rolled my eyes and called it old fogey entertainment, and now, I seek out those sounds because they remind me of home.

I can share with you the day I boldly challenged her, and told her she wouldn't *dare* spank me. She promptly did, but with a slight grin on her face because *she* knew, that *I* knew, it was a lesson I needed to learn.

I recall visiting Aunt Ailene's, feeling as though we were embarking on an adventurous road trip, though it was just a few miles down the road. And how *any* simple meal the two sisters cooked together turned into a feast. How their footsteps in the kitchen were as seamless as a symphony.

I remember sitting on Aunt Ethel's back porch, just looking for excuses to head down the stairs of the embankment and across the street to Doc Robertson's store. I must have bought hundreds of Dr. Peppers and Three Musketeers bars over the years, which were Uncle Harold's favorites. And banana popsicles for me.

Perhaps my favorite spot was the red swing on that big wraparound porch. We had so many discussions there. Me dangling my legs from that swing…and she, in the matching rocking chair. We talked about passing cars, school, family members, plans, and disappointments. She let me voice my opinion, only scolding me lightly whenever I cursed.

Most of all, I remember Sunday dinners. Her humble table was filled with dish after dish of southern cooking, along with one of her signature cakes or pies, sitting on top of the clothes dryer. I can still hear her saying, "I don't know if it will be fit to eat today". She was sincere when she said it, and it made me laugh—hard. Because I knew the ridiculousness of that statement.

I remember the small porcelain sink, perched on metal legs and barely attached to the wall, where we washed dishes after dinner. And I can still hear the clanging of the old aluminum wash pan that we filled with water to rinse them.

Every family member, and several of my closest friends, shared meals with me at the table in that small kitchen. And all were welcomed with an open heart. I'm sure everyone that walked through her door felt as I did. It felt like home, whether you were young or old. Successful or struggling. Lost or found. It was a refuge. A haven.

As the years went by, she took care of so many. She bravely and personally witnessed the final days and hours of several of her siblings, as well as her son. There seemed to be no end to her strength.

This is but a small window into the woman I know. So many things she did for me. So many lessons she taught me. And I know that I am *only one.* *Only one* of the lives she touched with her unassuming approach and unconditional acts of love.

I could keep you here for weeks telling you the stories and teachings of my interactions with her. But I know each of *you* has your own, and I would not be surprised to learn that they have shaped you, too.

After we leave here today, let us not forget the purity of the lessons she has taught us, and the depth of the kindness she has shown. When people say, "they don't make them like that anymore", I believe Aunt Ethel is the woman of whom they speak.

One speech will never honor her enough. And a thousand stories can only capture the still shots of a work that is no doubt still in progress. But if we each pay these memories and lessons forward in some small way, the seeds of her legacy could fill a forest with things 'they don't make any more'.

-Tonya Eberhart

CHAPTER 8:
Picking Up the Ball

Basketball began as an escape. I could walk outside, turn on my radio, and drown out the noise from the house. I could put down the misery, and pick up the ball. From the time that I was in the 7th grade, and throughout the years that I lived at Ethel's house, it became the center of my existence. It was my saving grace in more ways than one, because I rarely drank during basketball season. I was so focused on the sport, and didn't want to do anything that would keep me from playing.

Ford Phillips was the coach for my entire basketball career in school. In fact, he coached both the girls and boy's teams back then, and we didn't even have official teams until the 7th grade. Ford already had his eye on me by that time because I loved the game so much. In fact, when I was still living at the brick house, Ford let me come down and hang out at the gym. When he was practicing with the team on one end of the gym, I was shooting on the other. Then he'd take me back home and let me out at the bottom of the driveway.

Sometimes on the way home we'd stop by his daughter's house and I'd sit in the car while he went in briefly to talk with her. Later, after I began living at Ethel's, all I had was a motorcycle for transportation. So, in those first few years, if I didn't have a ride home after practice, Ford would give me a lift and drop me off in Ethel's driveway.

One day at school, it began to snow heavily, and continued until it was about six inches deep. They let school out as soon as they could, and I rode home with Ford in his Chevrolet. He didn't know how to drive in the slick snow, and he almost lost control.

As soon as I saw he was having trouble, I reached over and straightened the wheel out and told him, "when you start to slide this way, you have to turn the wheel this way. Don't mash the gas hard. Just a little." He appeared shaken and grateful, and all he could manage to say when we finally straightened up was, "Oh my goodness, the Lord was with us."

One of the most exciting times around the 8th grade year was when a new kid named Joe Thompson came to school. His family had been overseas because his Dad was in the military, and they moved back to Dawsonville, where Joe's Mom was originally from. He was in my grade, and was a phenomenal ball player.

We became fast friends, and we played so well together that Ford frequently asked us to scrimmage against the high school girls team. He was an insane ball handler and could shoot as good as I could. He could pass behind his back or between his legs and hit you dead on. We'd go up to the old elementary school (which later became a rubber plant) across the street from where Ethel lived and play on a dirt court.

Sadly, at the beginning of 9th grade, his family moved to Marietta, and it broke my heart when he moved because he was such a great player. He attended Sprayberry High School, one of the biggest schools in that area. Later, me and some friends went to watch him play ball one night.

He was twirling the ball on his finger all around the court during warmups. They had a 6'9" center, and in one signature move, all of a sudden Joe passed the ball like a bullet from behind his back. It hit his center perfectly, and he slammed it. It was quite a show. He ended up the 9th ranked player in the state at the end of his senior year. I'll always remember his talent and the impact his friendship made on my life, if even for a short time.

Soon after I moved to Ethel's, Herbert called me in the office one day and said, "Son, do you need a job?" I'm sure he knew times were hard. He said "I've got one for you that will be handy, and it will be honest. You can work around your basketball schedule, too." So, me and another student worked together cleaning, sweeping, and mopping in the cafeteria, and if there was time left over, we'd sweep and mop a few of the classrooms, and take out the trash. I worked two hours each weekday afternoon, and four hours each Saturday. It was convenient, because the girls team practiced first every afternoon right after school, followed by the boys around 5:00 p.m. That gave me a few hours to get the work done and make it to practice on time.

I was so grateful to have a job so I could have some spending money and feel like I was contributing, because Mama and Daddy had left us with nothing. But I was often tired, despite my high energy level. I remember fondly the kindness of Thelma Cox, our school librarian. She knew I worked all the time at the school, so on game days she let me sleep in the clinic during study hall and woke me up just before the bell rang for the next class.

This was my freshman year in high school, and to get a suit and be invited to play on the varsity team was an honor. It was one of the proudest moments of my life. Most freshmen wouldn't even try out for the varsity team because the chances of being chosen would be slim.

I was so excited that I barely thought twice as I put my basketball shoes on each day. The strings had broken, and I was lacing them together with a clothes hanger. One day Herbert called me to the office over the intercom. When I got there, he and Ford were the only two people in the office. They said, "Gene, we found these tennis shoes in the gym a couple of weeks ago, and no one has claimed them. Try them on, and if they fit you, you can have them." They were brand new, and exactly my size, a 9 ½.

I was so excited, it felt like Christmas. I remember walking back up the hallway with the box of shoes in my hands, thinking, "Why the hell would somebody buy a brand new pair of shoes and leave them behind?" At the time, brand new Converse All Stars were $16.00 at the Dawsonville Hardware store, but I just didn't have the money for them.

To those of you reading this right now, you may have already figured it out. But as an impressionable and somewhat gullible young kid, it didn't occur to me until years later that Herbert and Ford had bought those shoes especially for me.

This high school principal was the same man who took his two sons, along with me and a couple of other kids, to see the Beatles in 1964. They played at the Atlanta Braves stadium, and Herbert drove us there and sat in the parking lot while we enjoyed the show. During that era, principals all over the country hated the Beatles. But Herbert actually bought us tickets and took us to watch them play. The show was incredible, and each Beatle entered the baseball stadium in a separate limousine, one by one.

Of the top 10 songs in the nation at that time, I believe they had at least seven. On that baseball field, you can rightfully imagine that the acoustics weren't the best, but it's one of the most incredible concerts I've ever seen. They rocked the house.

Herbert would never seek credit for anything, not even the joy and salvation he brought into the lives of so many students, especially mine. He was just that good of a man. But I give him credit for every bit of guidance and love he showed toward me.

My first basketball game in 9th grade was against Woody Gap. This was the only time Mama and Daddy ever saw me play. It wasn't long before Daddy would be in prison. Ford put me in at the end of the game because we were way ahead, but I only played a minute or two. I was so nervous that I shot one time and it was an air ball. I remember being disappointed about that, but underneath it all I was just happy that I had a suit and I was on the team.

The rest of that year was pretty much the same story. I might get in a minute or two at the end of the game. Toward the end of the year, if our guys weren't shooting well, Ford would pull me off the bench and say, "Odom, nobody in there can shoot. Now, get that ball and shoot." But I didn't perform well that year. It was just too much pressure.

In my Sophomore year, I wish I could say things were different. I still wasn't a starter. Ford would tell me, "If you don't shoot, I'll pull you back out", and he did. I was still nervous, and couldn't seem to measure up to his expectations or mine. He was counting on me to go in the game and shoot like I did in practice, but my nerves took over, and I couldn't seem to make it happen. The year came and went rapidly.

During my junior year, we didn't have a really good team, but we were decent. Tragically, after our first game of that year, someone burned down the gym. The next morning, I received a call with the news, and it just made me sick. Right away, Forsyth County High School called us and said we could use their old gym for practice, which was in the middle of town. It was a lot like ours, a cracker box gym, which was nothing special. But at least we had a place to practice.

We got out of school about 30 minutes early each day, and Ford drove us in a bus to Cumming to practice. On the way to the gym, there was a funeral home, and he was forced to slow down quite a bit as we passed it. As soon as the bus slowed, a few of us boys would jump out the back door and head to a pool hall to play pool while the girls practiced. He never seemed to miss us, I guess because he was more focused on the girls' team that year, and dedicated most of practice time to them.

He practiced with the girls for a couple of hours, then the boys practiced for the final hour. The practice gym had a wood floor and metal backboards, but we arranged to play our games in their new gym, a dome shaped building that was modern for its time. It had a rubber floor and plexiglass backboards. That was the routine all throughout our junior year. We never played a home game, and the difference in the gyms certainly made a difference in our performance. Despite the change of venue and circumstances, that year is when all the tension left me and my determination truly kicked in. I averaged 22 points a game. I shot so well that everyone predicted I'd average 30 the next year.

We finally built a new gym and I believe we played our first game in it in December of 1965, near the beginning of our senior season. The new gym was bigger and nicer, except for the floor. The concrete wasn't poured level, and they put a rubber floor on top of it. When the ball hit the floor, you never really knew which direction it was going.

Ford continued to push me to shoot the ball. I remember feeling guilty at times because none of the other players even had a chance to shoot, but whenever I attempted to lay low and let someone else shoot, he would call a timeout and give me an earful. I knew what was required of me, but I honestly felt a little uncomfortable at times receiving all the glory when I felt the rest of the team deserved it, too.

The experience taught me to be proud of my accomplishments, but at the same time to show humility. Don't get me wrong, it felt amazing to be cheered on, encouraged and recognized everywhere I went. But I knew that I could only shoot if the rest of the team could handle the ball, pass the ball, and get it into my hands. There's no such thing as a one-man team.

During one momentous game, we were playing North Hall. I believe we were class C and they were class A back then. They had one big player on their team who was a smartass. They laughed at us when we came into their gym because they thought they were going to run us out. And I knew if I didn't score at least 30, we wouldn't have a chance.

At one point, we were 10-15 points behind, but we caught up in the last minute or so. With nine seconds left on the clock, there was a one point difference. North Hall was ahead, and we had the ball on their end of the court. They threw it to me, and I dribbled it to half court and shot it, knocking the bottom out of it.

My good friend Dennis Gilleland, who had already graduated, was at the game. He came running out, and yelled, "You lucky sonofabitch". I said, "Hell, I scored 25 or 30! How's that lucky?" But it *was* pure luck. I couldn't even see the goal. Three players were on me with their hands up. Luck just came at a good time.

There's a saying I often use to express victory: "We tore their dress". It was a scene any young athlete would remember for the rest of his life. The whole crowd came out of the stands and carried me off the court. I got so excited, I left my uniform in the dressing room that night. When I went back to North Hall Monday to pick it up, it was still wet and it smelled horrible. That's the only time I ever left my uniform behind.

I really believe it was meant to be for us to win because they were so cocky at the time. I don't believe we were good enough to ever beat them again. But it sure gave me a lot of satisfaction to do it even once.

When it finally came time for the tournaments my senior year, I was worn out. We had given it everything. I think we lost the second game in, and if memory serves me correctly, it was in Buford. I had so much on my mind then, and when it came time for the final game, I was actually sort of glad. I was just so tired.

Phil Jackson was a popular sports writer for *The Gainesville Times* back then, one of the most iconic of his time. It's entertaining and humbling now to look back at his descriptions of me as a ball player. He nicknamed me Odom One (like Air Force One), and it stuck for a while. Here are just a few excerpts from his articles:

"Gene Odum, Dawson County's human long range bomb sight, put on his best scoring performance of a banner scoring season last night to lead his Tigers to a 70-69 victory over Pickens County. Odum, who is averaging better than 30 points a game, snapped the nets for 43 points."

"Odum Bombs Beat Buford For Dawson...There may be a better shooter in Georgia prep basketball circles

than Gene Odum, but Dawson County fans will argue that point with anyone who cares to listen."

"Odum bombed the nets for 34 points and this is close to the figure he is averaging through nine games this season. Veteran Dawson Coach Ford Phillips says Odum is one of the finest shotmakers he has ever seen in his long cage career."

"Dawson County's Gene Odum has received honorable mention on the Coach & Athlete Magazine's Prep All-America basketball team. Odom, a graduating senior, led Georgia in scoring with an average of more than 30 points a game while starring for Coach Ford Phillips' Dawson County Tigers."

I saw Phil Jackson years later and got to know him pretty well. Every time our paths crossed, he would yell across the room, "Odum, come over here!" All those years later, it still felt great to be recognized, and I consider myself fortunate to have been covered by such a respected sports writer.

After he passed away, I was given this letter that Phil wrote to Charles Finley, a great friend and classmate, who was doing a project on the history of basketball in Dawson County. Charles had asked Phil to contribute to the project, and here is the letter he wrote when he agreed to contribute.

Dear Mr. Finley,

I have some very pleasant memories of writing about and broadcasting Dawson County High School basketball in past years.

For more than 30 years I was sports editor of The Times and during that period Coach Ford Phillips was one of my favorite figures in coaching.

Always cooperative and always up-tempo about his teams, Coach Phillips was a colorful and successful coach.

I remember that one of Dawson County's biggest wins ever came in the 1960's against an undefeated Jackson County team in the region tournament at Buford.

I broadcast that game on radio and remember I attempted to interview Coach Phillips after the win. But he was so excited he grabbed the microphone from my hands and basically interviewed himself as he praised the efforts of his team.

Dawson County had some memorable players. I especially recall Nicky Gilleland, Eugene Odum, Woody Bowen, and Jimmy Phillips, Coach Phillips' son.

No doubt, Eugene Odum to this day ranks as the best outside shooter I ever saw in basketball. And this includes pros

*such as Larry Bird and any college player I
ever saw.*

   *Thank you for this opportunity to
contribute to your project on the history
of Dawson County High School
basketball.*

   Sincerely,
   Phil Jackson
   The Times
   Gainesville, Ga.

I knew Daddy got the *Atlanta Journal & Constitution*
while he was in prison, and he must have seen my
write-ups, but he never mentioned it. Ethel always got
the *Gainesville Times*, and I had a write-up almost
weekly during my junior and senior years. For a young
kid from humble beginnings, it was a big deal to be
featured in any newspaper. But in any case, neither
of my parents ever asked me about basketball.

I couldn't possibly complete this chapter without
mentioning my biggest fan of all, Clyde Wallace. He
not only attended every single game, he kept my stats
for every game I played my junior & senior years. He
was so precise that he would often correct the
official statisticians. And he was one of the most
generous people I've ever known.

For a few months, I actually lived with Clyde and his
family. He knew our living quarters were tight at

Ethel's, and he offered me a bed to sleep in, which sounded pretty good to me.

He also took an entire weekend to fix my car, which by now was getting some age and wear on it. He never asked me for a dime. I can remember the night I drove the car out of the garage. It was so cold that I could hear the crunch of the tires on the frozen ground. I remember thinking that I had a good transmission and good tires, and it felt safe. I was so proud to have it. Clyde has since passed away, but I'll never forget his generosity and dedication, and I owe him a huge debt of gratitude.

At the end of the season, I was greeted with another surprise. Daryl Robinson (Herbert's son) walked up to me and handed me a stack of papers. It was all the articles that had been written about me as a player. He never told me he was collecting them, and the fact that he saved those meant so much to me. The excerpts in this chapter were taken word for word from those articles.

We had a winning season in our senior year. I was the top scoring player in the state of Georgia, averaging 31 points a game, and ranked an overall 7th in the state. My highest score in a single game was 43 points. To my knowledge and those whom I've consulted, I still hold that record for the highest average scoring season *without* three point lines. I got college letters from all over the U.S. asking me to try out for their teams. I couldn't even read them all, and ended up throwing most of them away. The only places I actually tried out or visited were at Berry College in Mt Berry and Brewton-Parker College in Mount Vernon, Georgia. I did extremely well in the Berry College tryout, and when we left, Ford informed me that I would have a full ride scholarship if I decided to attend.

I was on top of the world, and for the first time, I felt as though things were looking up for me. I couldn't imagine a better scenario. I was the star of the team, colleges were attempting to recruit me, and I could get a free education doing the one thing I loved most in the world. I had escaped the chaos, and my future was bright.

But I'm sure you could guess by now that this part of the story doesn't end with me playing college basketball in an arena full of thousands of fans. During my senior year I had been dating someone from my class, and mid-season, I found out that we were expecting a baby.

It seemed as though every time I could see a star, it fizzled out before my eyes. It was just a mirage that kept me moving in a single direction, but as I got closer, it seemed to disappear. This was a whole new ballgame. A hard decision had to be made, and once again it would change the course of my life.

CHAPTER 9:
Detour & Destiny

Throughout my junior and senior years, I dated Kay Reagan. Kay had moved to Dawsonville from Atlanta in 1963. I believe one of the things that connected us was a history of tragedy. Kay was only 14 when her parents both died on the same day in 1962. Her father had a history of mental illness, and soon after returning from one of several stints at a mental hospital, he shot and killed her mother, then turned the gun on himself. Kay was one of seven children, and in a single fateful moment, all of their lives would be turned upside down.

The children were immediately dispersed among various family members throughout different parts of Georgia. Two of them (the only two boys, Ronnie and Randy) would stay with family members for only a short while before being sent to an orphanage. Ronnie was the oldest, and escaped from the orphanage when he was 16 to live on his own. Randy, one of the youngest children, would remain in the orphanage for another 3 years. There were some similarities in our lives with regard to hardships and pain, and I think that's one of the things that drew us to one another.

Kay's cousin first introduced us during our junior year, and we dated on and off for a couple of years. Our first date was actually a double date with my good friend David Disharoon, and Kay's cousin, Vickie. I had just traded my motorcycle for a 1955 Chevrolet. David and I had worked on it throughout the summer, putting on a new fender and bumper, and David's Dad painted it for me.

I didn't know it until almost 30 years later, but the motor in that car was actually stolen from Ford Phillips. Apparently, someone had stolen Ford's car a couple of years earlier. The car was later found abandoned with our team basketballs still in the trunk, and the motor was missing. Hot motors were common back then, for sure, but I never thought about it even once. I would have been horrified to know it at the time. It was the first time I had something really nice to drive.

Kay asked if she could drive it during our first date, and I handed over the wheel. Within the first couple of miles, she wrecked and turned it over. It happened so quickly, and I'll never forget the feeling when the car flipped. It was a trip car before I got it, and it had springs and shocks that made the car sit level and sturdy for hauling liquor. Unfortunately, that made it much easier to flip. When it turned onto its top, it felt just like we were riding on cotton balls.

Thankfully, no one was hurt, and we just flipped it back over, put the battery back in, and finished our date. I never said a word to Kay, but I was just sick about it. The humorous side of that event is that, a week later, David and I wrecked and rolled it again, totaling it this time.

We found out that Kay was pregnant in February of our senior year. Shortly afterward, she quit school. She sacrificed a lot, and even returned to school the following year to finish her degree. As for me, I knew I had a huge decision to make at the time, too.

I had three options. I could go to Vietnam (I was already classified 1-A), I could go to college and be exempt from Vietnam, or I could get married and take care of my wife and child. The fact that a child was on the way would also exempt me from going to Vietnam. I was constantly plagued with worry about this decision. In fact, the only time I wasn't worrying was when I was immersed in playing ball.

Many of my friends were preparing to leave for Vietnam after graduation, and I remember feeling guilty because I felt like that's what I should be doing, too. However, I'd be lying if I didn't say I was somewhat relieved that I had other options. I remember the stress of this decision. I'm not sure exactly why I didn't choose to do both--raise a family and go to college. I assume it's because I just didn't have the support system. There was no back up plan, and no one who could help us financially. And finally, I just wanted to do the right thing.

I went on our Senior Trip that year to Washington DC, and as soon as the train arrived back near home, I knew what I had to do. Kay and I made plans to get married right away. I'm dumbfounded that I don't even remember anything about leaving Ethel's to meet Kay and get married. I don't remember packing or saying good-bye. I got back from the senior trip on June 3rd, and we were married on June 6th.

Kay's Aunt Geneva and Uncle Brice had been her guardians since her parents died, and they went along with us. We drove to Winder and we were married in a small courthouse there, which is still standing today.

After we got married, we moved to Monticello with Kay's Uncle Bud, intending to live there at least until the baby was born. He owned a beer joint just off a main road where the railroad tracks intersected. One memory sticks out to me during that time. There was a church about 100 yards away from the beer joint and on the other side of the tracks. Bud would ask me to walk down the driveway on Sundays and see if church had let out yet. When I could see people leaving the church, I'd let him know. He'd say, "Well, I'd better open up, because they'll be thirsty now." And sure enough, quite a few of them would head straight to the beer joint after church.

It was July, and I remember that it was insufferably hot at the time, and Kay was miserable. In fact, we both were miserable. She was approaching nine months of pregnancy, and she just couldn't take it any longer. We went to the doctor and told him we'd heard that if you take castor oil, it could cause you to go into labor. We asked if that would hurt her or the baby. He said, "You can try it, but I don't think it will work."

So, we headed straight home and Kay took a whole bottle of castor oil with a Coke. We walked for about two and a half hours, then she started having labor pains. I got her to the hospital as quickly as I could, but not fast enough for pain medicine, so it was a natural birth. At 2:29 in the afternoon on July 31st, Tonya was born. The doctor called Kay his "little trooper".

Boy, was it a surreal feeling to be a Dad. Although I'll never forget the elation, I still felt like I was ill equipped for the job of being a father. Right after Tonya was born, we went to live with Kay's grandmother (we called her Ma Ma) in Lithonia for a little while, at least until we could get on our feet and get our own place.

Ma Ma's house was an old wooden plank home with an enclosed breezeway separating the two halves of the house. Ronnie (Kay's brother) and his wife, Joanne, were also living there at the same time. They lived in one half of the house and we lived in the breezeway in a makeshift bedroom surrounded by curtains.

Ronnie and Joanne also had a new baby. We were just two kids trying to raise two kids. We wondered how we'd ever make it out of this situation. Ronnie didn't even have a car before we arrived, and I'm not even sure how he was making it all work.

My cousin Mickey got me and Ronnie a job as trim helpers for a contractor. We toted doors up the steps of a warehouse and used a hacksaw to cut galvanized pipe for closet hangers. We did it for a week and didn't make a penny because the guy went bankrupt. Then I went to work for a plumbing company in Riverdale.

I was driving a 1957 Ford back then, and it was getting worn out. One day we were headed down the expressway to work, and you could hear a flapping noise. The rear end was going out. I can't remember the details of how we got our hands on a newer one, but I know we did it on credit and paid for it at the end of the week. We drove two wheels up onto the sidewalk in front of Ma Ma's house and made just enough room to squeeze underneath the car. We didn't have any mechanic's tools to work with, so we just made do with what we had. We put the rear end in the car right there on the side of the road.

On Sundays, we'd sit in the rocking chairs on Ma Ma's front porch. While most teenagers were out having fun, we didn't have a single penny to spend on fun. Our idea of fun happened on an occasional

Friday night, when we were able to scrounge together enough money to head to Burger King for a Whopper. We thought we'd hit the jackpot because most of our meals were beans in those days.

These living arrangements didn't last long, however. Shortly after Tonya was born, I learned that my best friend, Dennis Gilleland, had been killed in a car accident. He was working at Lockheed at the time, and was carpooling to work with two other guys. The morning of the accident, he was headed to work, and realized he had forgotten his badge, so they turned back around to get it, and that's when the accident happened. Both Dennis and Bubba Bearden were killed.

Dennis was a Senior when I was a Junior, and we had played basketball together. He ran the offense, but didn't shoot very much. During a game, people would yell at him to "shoot the ball!", but he just replied with, "I don't have to. I've got this boy right here to shoot." Then he'd pass the ball to me.

I was devastated. We went back home to Dawsonville for the funeral, and that's when things became very clear to me. I needed to be back home. In Atlanta, I didn't know who to trust. I needed to get back to a place where I knew the people and everything was familiar again. In Dawsonville, I knew everyone, from mechanics to people who ran local businesses, and friends that would come to the rescue for any occasion.

It was a scary time. I was homesick and lost. I had already been responsible for myself since I had been living at Ethel's, but now this was different. I went from the glory and praise of my basketball years to becoming responsible for not only myself, but caring for a wife and child in a place where I knew no one. Above all, I faced the sudden realization that this was the end of *my* childhood.

Although this detour was not what I had imagined, I had come to accept that I was a Dad now, and my family depended on me. I never wanted to look back and say that I didn't provide, and I never wanted my children to experience the uncertainty that had become a way of life for me. I could do better for them. But in order to do that, I would need a support system...of any kind. They say you can never return home. But when it's all you know, when it encompasses your entire existence, the good and the bad, you do the thing you know. And I knew my destiny would begin with returning home.

CHAPTER 10:
Returning Home

Once we returned home, we struggled for the first few years. We moved a lot during that time, bouncing from rental to rental. We lived in a trailer just off Highway 53 near Perimeter Road, a small apartment near the Dawsonville Pool Room and a house behind the high school football field, to name a few. Money was so tight that I remember asking Doc Robertson to pump just a quarter's worth of gas, which was about a quarter a gallon back then, and that would get me to Dawsonville and back.

Although we were struggling, at least we were surrounded by people who could help when we really needed it. I borrowed Gordon Pirkle's truck several times to move furniture. Gordon is a Dawsonville icon, and the owner of the Dawsonville Pool Room. He's also a racing enthusiast and responsible for the launch and operation of the Georgia Racing Hall of Fame. I knew I could always count on his support.

Many friends and acquaintances over the years let me borrow things or buy from them on credit until I could pay it off. They knew Daddy was good for his word, and they knew I would be, too. The moonshine code runs deep.

Daddy had been transferred from Tallahassee to Atlanta by this time, and was allowed out during the day on work release. This was common back then because they wanted the inmates to be prepared to reenter the workforce upon their sentence completion. He left the prison in the morning with a packed lunch and worked all day, then returned at night. He was a construction laborer in a high rise building right above The Varsity in Atlanta. He also occasionally worked for the warden at his home, cutting grass and doing other chores.

One day I took Kay and Tonya with me to his work site to visit. He was on the 5th floor of the building, and was allowed to take a lunch break to spend a little time with us. I believe this was the first time he'd ever seen Tonya, but I could be mistaken on the details. I do, however, vividly recall the series of events that took place after he had served his four years and had finally been released.

Times were hard, and as is often the case, old habits die hard, too. As a struggling family man, I kept leaning back on the only jobs I'd ever really known, so when one of Daddy's old liquor buddies approached me to work on his still, I agreed. He knew I needed a job, and he knew Daddy would, too, as soon as he was released.

The still was inside an old brick house right on a creek, where Buford Highway and I-285 intersect. Back then, moonshiners found houses like this because they were contract rentals. Property managers rented them out for the owners.

I didn't even know how to make liquor, I was just familiar with the jobs and the culture. The still was so huge that several men could stand inside it at once. When you moved it, it would make a loud rumbling sound that the neighbors could hear. My job was to build the plywood boxes that held the mash. The dimensions were 4'x4'x4', and we had to have enough boxes to run seven days a week, producing 300 gallons a day, at any given time in the basement. Being made of wood, they leaked at first, but once they swelled up with the mash, they didn't leak any more.

I had been working on the still about a week before Daddy was released. The day I picked him up from prison, the plan was to head straight to the still. Coming up the road, I said, "Daddy, are you sure you want to do this? Four years is a long time". He responded in his usual somber tone, "Where else am I gonna go? I need the money". We both felt we didn't have any other option.

The still was managed by an older couple who were hired to work at the site. He kept an eye on the property, and she cooked for the workers, which was usually just soup beans, onions and cornbread. We worked about 18 hours a day.

Some of the guys on the still would run materials and liquor back and forth in a van. One day just a couple of weeks into the job, I was watching out the window as our driver pulled away from the site. I watched him get onto Buford Hwy, headed toward I-285. A minute or so later, I saw the same van coming back. I said to Daddy, "He's coming back. He forgot something." And as I leaned forward to get a better look out of the big picture window of the living room, I saw a man wearing a suit with a badge on it. I immediately yelled, "It's time to go."

My flight response kicked into high gear, and I burst out the back door, knocking two revenue officers down. I was just out of school and in good physical shape. I could run forever. As I approached the creek, there was a barbed wire fence ahead, and I scaled it, never touching it. The officers stopped at the fence, and I thought, "Hell, I've got this. I'm gonna get away."

As I approached the creek to cross it, I knew that wading it would slow me down, so I decided to dive in. I couldn't tell how deep it was because it had been raining and the creek was so muddy. As I dove in it almost knocked me out because it was only about a foot deep. I grabbed onto a root to pull myself out of the water, and I was looking down the barrel of a pistol. There were officers lined up down the creek, one about every 20 feet.

They handcuffed me, and started walking back toward the house. In order to get back there, we either had to cross I-285 or walk across a sewer line, a few feet above the water level. I was trying to think of any way I could possibly escape. I glanced downward at the slope and for a split-second thought about pushing the revenue officer into the creek, but he was handcuffed to me. I didn't have a chance.

Once we got back to the house, they began questioning all of us. When they asked me my name, I said my name was Jimmy Johnson from Jefferson, Georgia. That answer wasn't really planned. It's just the way it came out. A few minutes went by and one of the revenue officers looked at me and said, "When are you gonna tell the truth? I know your name is not Jimmy Johnson, boy. I watched you play ball."

Five of us were put into the paddy wagon and the guy who shoved me in hit my head. They transported us to the police station. It was a big bust, and all three major TV networks were there. It was also covered in the Dekalb County newspaper. Walking to and from the wagon, I pulled my coat over my head, hoping no one could see my face on TV. I remember being glad that I had recently grown a beard, which might further my disguise. Foremost in my mind, I didn't want Herbert Robinson to see that moment, to know that I had fallen so far, and made such a catastrophic mistake.

I was the only one that even got out the door that day. Daddy never even tried, and was handcuffed immediately. He had only been out of prison a few weeks. We found out later that there had been another still there before that one, so we were unknowingly doomed from the start.

The friend who had hired us for the job made our bond and they let all of us go. The bail bondsman picked us up and took us straight to a stash house where we had the liquor stored. It was in a nice home near Six Flags, and far from the site of the still. We had so much liquor there that the floor was falling in.

During the operation of the still, the liquor would go from the stash house straight to the shot houses in Atlanta, often still warm when it arrived. I remember being angry about stopping at the stash house, because we'd just gotten out of jail, and didn't need any more trouble. I never did understand why he took us there.

Thankfully, I was home by 11:00 that night, and I saw myself on the news, but no one else knew it was me. I was horrified by the choices I had made, and I swore I'd never be involved in that kind of lifestyle again.

I lived on edge for weeks after that, and one day I received a summons to report to court for arraignment. I immediately reached out to Daddy's friend who had hired us, expressing my concern and asking for advice on representation and how to handle the case. He told me not to worry about it, to tear up the notice. He was insistent. Turns out, he knew people in positions of power, and paid $10,000 to have the case thrown out for all five of us. I also learned years later that a party was held to burn all the evidence, including the photos, at the home of someone in high places.

That was probably the luckiest moment of my life. It was also when I decided I'd never again be involved in any manner with the liquor business. I felt defeated, and embarrassed. I hitchhiked to Gainesville one day and managed to get a job hauling frozen chickens for a few weeks, but I hated it. The truck I was driving was in dire need of repairs, and the brakes almost went out coming down Blood Mountain. That was the trigger for me.

That day, I went back to Gainesville and turned in the truck. I told them I wasn't going to drive a death trap into the mountains, and I had decided to find another job. I was worn out and pissed off about life. I got out of the car near a telephone booth, and in desperation, called the only person I knew I could count on. Herbert Robinson.

He answered with a genuine tone, glad to hear from me. "Son, how are you?" I was about to cry. I was so ashamed because I'd been caught making liquor and I didn't know whether he knew it. I said, "I'm not doing too good, Herbert. I need a job. A good job."

Without pausing, he asked, "Where are you?" I told him I was in a phone booth in Gainesville. He said, "Give me the number, and stay right there and wait for me to call back." Within ten minutes, he called and said, "Go to Chicopee on Atlanta Highway and talk to Harold Brooks. He's the Personnel Manager there, and I think he might have something for you."

I was hired that very day, and my first job was operating a printing machine, printing things like labels and checks. The job was cool in the summer and warm in the winter, and I'd never had that before. I was so grateful, and it was then that I realized the full impact Herbert had on my life. It was life transforming every time we interacted, ever since the third grade. Ten minutes here and ten minutes there. Every ten minutes he spent with me, it was like I learned ten years' worth of wisdom. That day in Gainesville was the last time I called on him for help.

Herbert was the Dean of Students at Gainesville Junior College, which was just down the road from Chicopee. He would occasionally go to the mall to eat and walk during lunchtime. One of my most satisfying moments was the day I ran into him there. I was dressed up in nice clothes, and he asked me, "How are you doing, Gene? Are you still working at Chicopee?" I said, "Ten years." And all he said was, "Good boy."

Kay ended up working at Chicopee, too, for a few years. She was assigned to the baby products division from 1967 to 1970. She was a hard worker, a good mother, and tough as nails. She had been through so much, too, including the splintering of her family in one fell swoop. Family was always important to her, and the thought of her younger brother, Randy, still in an orphanage, was weighing heavily on her heart.

After the death of her parents, Randy and Ronnie had eventually ended up in Clinton, SC at Thornwell Presbyterian Orphanage. Ronnie just left one day and never came back. Randy remained there for a few years after that, so as soon as Kay was old enough to get him out, we borrowed $300 to pay the court costs and present our case before a judge in Gainesville in order to become his temporary guardians.

He was twelve years old when we went to get him out. I thought he was one of the most beautiful children I'd ever seen. We were all so proud that day. I took him a football, and we could tell it meant so much to him. He was excited to be going home with us, and kept leaning over the back of the seat during the ride, talking a mile a minute about everything.

He lived with us for a couple of years, and his creativity and mischievousness no doubt helped to prepare us for parenthood. After we had celebrated Tonya's first birthday, we kept a piece of her birthday cake in the freezer as a memento of the occasion. When I came home from work one night, I opened the freezer and noticed the piece of cake was missing.

When I walked into the living room, I could see the edge of a saucer that had been shoved underneath the couch. Knowing that Randy was a crafty child who had a million excuses, I went to him and said, "What's that on your mouth? It looks like icing." His face immediately went white, and he knew he was busted. For the record, though, there was no icing on his face.

On another such creative occasion, I had left for work one morning but had forgotten something, so I had to turn around and head back home. On the way, I met our old Pontiac on the road, with Randy at the wheel. He had taken off the entire dashboard in order to straight wire it. I found out later that he had been driving it for weeks before he was caught.

We had quite a few challenges throughout his time with us, some more serious than others, but all of them were the result of a shattered childhood. Regardless, I'm glad we took him in and did what we could to give him a home if even for a short time. It turns out we would have similarities in our struggles throughout the years ahead.

After we got married, I also reunited with Mama. The man she was dating helped us buy our first home in early 1970. The home was perfect for us, located on a hill along Hwy 9 in Dawsonville, which would later become known as Thunder Road. We bought ten acres, which included a chicken house and another building that was used for cleaning eggs and storage. It also came with a trailer next to the house, which eventually became a home for Mama. Kay and

Mama got along famously, and worked together in the chicken house for a couple of years before we stopped raising chickens.

Shortly after we bought the house, we found out we were expecting another child. We knew we wanted a boy and a girl, and we were hoping this one would be a boy. The day Kay's water broke, I called Brice and Geneva again, and they rode with me to take her to Northeast Georgia Medical Center. We rolled her into the emergency room in a wheelchair, and parted ways at the delivery waiting room door.

I'll never forget the men in the waiting room that night. Five or six of them were sitting there, unshaven, looking like they had been dragged through hell. They gave me some advice right away. "You might as well sit down, you're in for a long haul." Some of them had been there for 24 hours. I told Brice we might as well go get something to eat, because I was starving. We went to Waffle House next to the Holiday Inn, and took our time.

As soon as we arrived back at the hospital, I heard my name over the intercom, instructing me to come to the delivery waiting room. When I got there, a nurse told me that the doctor was looking for me. He said, "You have a son." I'll never forget the look on the faces of the other men in the waiting room. It was like, "Sonofabitch, he just got here a couple of hours ago, and we've been here forever".

On September 1st, 1970, at 10:24pm, Michael was born. His hair was so black it looked blue, and he was a beautiful child. My heart was full, and life was looking up. For the first time in a long time, it began to feel like family.

Strangely enough, Mama became pregnant at the same time Kay was pregnant with Michael, and my half-sister, Sherri, was born on November 8th of the same year. Though we still struggled from time to time to make ends meet, it was home, and it was nice to have the kids growing up together.

We helped Daddy rent some land on Dawson Forest Road after we put the case behind us. We put a camper trailer on it, and gave him some beer to bootleg so he could make a little money. Shortly afterward, he met a woman named Mamie, and they ended up getting married. For the next 40 years, we would only see Daddy once or twice a year.

This moment in time was the beginning of the ten calmest and happiest years of my life. It was indeed nice to be home. Home never leaves you, regardless of the miles or the circumstances. It's in your soul, and a resounding factor that is present in every thought, action, and decision. And just when you think you've got it made, just when you step out of the hole and into the light, other choices await you. All of my life up until then, I had fought someone else's demons. Now, it was time to fight my own.

CHAPTER 11:
Fateful & Futile Directions

I wish I could say that I learned from the mistakes of my parents. I certainly wish I could say that their demons didn't leave footsteps for me to follow absentmindedly. I wish I could say that I took the straight and narrow path. But of course, this book would have little interest had I learned so easily. I took an entirely different direction, yet I ended up on the same path that I had loathed my entire existence.

My journey with alcohol began with the fated Busch Bavarian in a coffee mug. For the next decade, I drank now and again, but not heavily. I partied like most twenty something's do, and for the first several years of married life, I gradually slid down the proverbial slippery slope. I was already taking speed, like Black RJS, right out of school. Then Speckled Bird. These were known as truck driver pills. They gave me energy, and made me feel the beginnings of invincibility.

Although I was willing to take the pills, ironically, I was still committed to staying as far away from the illegal activities of moonshine as possible. But financially, things were still tight, and I was looking to make extra money. A friend asked me if I knew anyone who had any milk jugs. "What for?", I asked. He replied, "Liquor". The moonshiners were changing from glass containers (Ball mason jars) to plastic because revenuers were getting wise to their sources, and they needed another solution. They couldn't stop the flow of sugar because it was a commodity people had to have, so they interfered with the flow of mason jars in an attempt to slow down the business. He told me if I'd help him find some plastic jugs, I could make a spread. He'd give me a quarter for each jug. It doesn't sound like big money, but when you sell them by the thousands, it becomes a business.

I wondered, where do you get used milk jugs? The trash dump was my first thought. But the objective was to get my hands on them before they made it that far. As luck would have it, on my way to work one morning, I noticed a big pile of milk jugs in someone's yard. I stopped in, and sure enough, the elderly couple that lived in the home was selling them. They had even developed a rudimentary system for cleaning them by using a cloth attached to a clothes hanger that could clean the jug and run through the jug handle, too.

If that wasn't fate, I also found out that their son worked for a garbage company. I struck a deal with both of them. Whenever the son picked up garbage, he tossed the milk jugs aside and brought them home. Then, his parents would clean them. I paid the son a nickel for the jugs, and the parents a nickel for the cleaning, so they cost me a dime each.

Allow me to put this in perspective. Back then, I was making $1.40 an hour at Chicopee. That's $56.00 per week. I stopped by that house a couple of times a week at first and picked up a load of jugs, then it became four to five days a week once I convinced the couple to get more jugs from their network and sources. I picked up about 300 jugs almost every weekday just from that location. I sold them for a quarter, pocketing fifteen cents each. Just at that volume, I was making $45.00 per day, and that's pretty much what paid for our house.

Within six months to a year, most of the people who made liquor in Dawson County bought their jugs from me. I became known as "The Jug Man". I stored the jugs in the chicken house, where I tied 25 of them to a string and sold them by the bundle. The empty jugs made a sound just like thunder when you moved them around.

It wasn't against the law to purchase or haul empty milk jugs. It was, however, against the law to deliver them to a still. So, I told my customers I'd bring them within a mile of the still, but no closer. I dropped thousands of them almost exactly one mile from multiple stills throughout the county. Beyond needing the money, I figured this was an opportunity to continue the business with the Odom name and preserve a part of my family legacy without the fear or risk of getting caught and building time.

In all that time in the jug business, I thankfully never got caught. There was one moment of doubt, however, when I was making a delivery one night and some guys who were working on the still jumped out to surprise me. I suddenly realized that my drop-off location was only thirty yards from the still. The operator of the still had ignored the fact that I said I didn't want to deliver that closely, and believe me, we had words about that. If I had been caught, I'd have gone to jail for conspiracy.

The Jug Man operation gave me financial stability that I had never had before. It felt great not worrying about making the mortgage, fixing the cars, or providing clothes and shoes for two growing kids.

But when an impressionable mind senses contentment, good never seems to be good enough. Having money back then was the first part of things going wrong at home. When you hear people say, "Money is the root of all evil", I understand the concept. However, I'm not going to blame it on the money. Actually, the problem begins when you *love* the money and allow the money to change you, to affect your values and decisions. But I didn't have that enlightened view at the time.

I'd be lying if I said we didn't enjoy the lifestyle the money provided. We bought things for the house and we went out on the weekends. We were living more than comfortably. I was beginning to let it get to my head, and felt like it was time for the next level, the next phase. Indeed, enough was never enough.

Then a plane crashed at Lockheed. It was a pot plane attempting a big delivery. I used to hear it fly over the house on Sunday nights. It flew so low, it vibrated the house. Before this event, I had never even seen pot before. And after the plane crash, it seemed like everyone in Dawsonville had it.

The law attempted to burn it on site the night the plane crashed, but it wouldn't burn. It was too compressed, so they took it to the city dump and dug a deep hole and buried it. A bunch of local boys found out about it and went to the dump that same night and dug it up. Within weeks, these guys were driving nicer cars, buying motorcycles, and spending money like water.

They were selling it for over $100 a pound, and some people in Atlanta were even paying $300 a pound. It became a booming enterprise, and when the pot ran low in Dawsonville, they'd go to Florida and pick up more or have it flown in from Colombia. It was much more profitable than moonshine, and it spread fast. The locals also loved it.

I had a relative who was involved in the whole operation from the beginning, but I didn't know it at the time. He approached me one day and asked, "Do you have anything in that chicken house?" He told me he had an old truck and a van that he needed to park somewhere. Since we weren't raising chickens any more, I agreed to let him park the vehicles there.

After the arrangement, though, my paranoid and curious mind began to wander. I certainly didn't need any more trouble, and I wanted to make sure he wasn't storing liquor or supplies, so one day I went to the chicken house and opened the vehicle doors to look inside. All I found was a Miami newspaper and a lot of lights and batteries. That satisfied my curiosity, and I felt relieved.

I noticed that he showed up a few Sunday nights to get the vehicles out. One Sunday night, I heard the plane flying low over the house again. And then word came that a plane had crashed on the west side of the county. I can't be sure it was the same night the vehicles were moved, but it did make me think. I began to put two and two together, and had made a decision to tell him not to bring the vehicles back.

It turns out, he never brought them back after that night anyway, so I never had to have that conversation. I found out later that the batteries and lights were probably used for a portable drop zone for the plane. He apparently needed the vehicles close by for a drop, and that's the only time they were ever moved. He never told me that's what he was doing.

Of course, I eventually fell in line with the rest of the experimenters and tried smoking pot, but it made me so paranoid, I couldn't stand it. It just wasn't my thing. It did, however, open one more taboo doorway, which led to another. Then another. I was immersed in the lifestyle, and I was gone a lot. My focus was on escaping reality and making money.

Combined with a lot of bad choices, it ruined my marriage. I felt like I had been cheated out of my youth by having to get married so young. Today, I know that I was a man without wisdom or principled examples, and I simply made mistakes. Big ones. And after the divorce, they began to grow even bigger. The events I'm sharing in this story are not for the purpose of aggrandizing them, but to show the colossal mess I'd gotten myself into.

In the years that followed, I wrecked almost as many cars as Daddy had, beginning with a green Toyota truck. I was going canoeing one day, and I was driving the truck to the exit point. I was always a stickler for a spotless car, and had a habit of putting Armor All on the seats.

When I was rounding a curve, an eight-track tape slid across the slippery seat and fell into the floorboard. I reached down to try and catch it and wrecked, almost turning the truck over. My knee was trapped underneath the steering wheel, and I couldn't break free.

I was on Quaaludes that day, and had a bag of them with me. I knew once the police showed up, they'd find them, so I started eating them, and what I couldn't eat, I started throwing out the window. That was merely the beginning of my foolish choices.

After speed came the cocaine. I was first introduced to it in 1980, when the Georgia Bulldogs went to New Orleans for the National Championship. A few friends and I bought a quarter ounce to take with us to the Sugar Bowl, and we stayed up four days straight during that trip. Cocaine has a numbing effect. It peps you up like speed for short periods, maybe an hour. It feels like utopia. It's a rich man's drug, and it makes you spend money like you had a lot of it. I stayed on it until 1986, pretty much every day.

Then I started freebasing it. I went to a friend's house one day and he was cooking cocaine on his stove. "We're trying this freebasing", he said. You cook cocaine down to its purest form. It's a rock, and you can put it in a pipe and smoke it. It's totally different than snorting it. It makes you really high, really quick. And real paranoid. When I started freebasing, that's when I really went downhill. It's the most addictive thing I've ever touched, and I wouldn't touch it again for a million dollars. It's made for the hard addict...or it makes a hard addict. It hits your brain in two seconds.

I got so bad that I couldn't function without the drugs. I would cut out a line on the nightstand beside my bed before I fell asleep, and when the clock went off,

I'd snort it and lay back down until it hit me so I could go to work.

But just like Newton's third Law of Motion, all actions have an equal and opposite reaction. And the reaction was life changing. The management at Chicopee noticed the change, and started doing urine testing. They called my hand, and then came the reaction, or verdict. "Go to treatment or go home". I had hit bottom, and I agreed to go to treatment for a chance at some normalcy.

I couldn't keep up with the speed, meaning the drugs and the pace. It was too much, and my body was dwindling. I knew I was facing death if I stayed on that path. I agreed to attend what was then the Charlotte Treatment Center in Charlotte, North Carolina.

The person who drove me to Charlotte was the first and only drug counselor for Chicopee, which was owned by Johnson & Johnson. He was a recovering addict himself, and I believe he had a doctorate degree. He was a kind man, and never judged me. I'll never forget the three and a half hour ride to Charlotte. I recall feeling numb, staring out the window. I had three or four Quaaludes in my pocket, and when we stopped to get something to eat, I took them. I wanted to feel that feeling one last time before checking in.

At one point, I looked at the counselor and said, "There's not a bit of need to take me up here. I don't have an addiction. I'm just crazy". And I believed every syllable of it. I didn't realize that the drugs were causing the feelings I had or the position I was in. Hell, I was freebasing cocaine until 3 or 4am, and then going to work. I was about dead, but I still didn't connect the dots. I had always been surrounded by crazy, and I honestly believed that was the entirety of my problem.

When we arrived at Charlotte Treatment Center, they happened to be hosting an annual conference there. There were hundreds of addicts in attendance from all over the country, and this event just happened to take place while I was there. They bussed us to an auditorium. Some guy got on stage, and said, "I'm an addict and alcoholic, and I want to tell you a little about my story."

He grew up around horse tracks, and got into gambling, then drinking. He was good at gambling, and became pretty well off. But he kept drinking until he lost his touch, his family, everything. He said, "I was living in a cardboard box. One day I woke up with someone knocking on the flap of my box, which was behind the bar. He said, 'Mr. White, we're here to repossess your Cadillac.' That's when I realized I had hit rock bottom, and I said to him, 'Do you think I care if you take my Cadillac? I'm living in a box behind a bar, with no teeth.'"

Although the circumstances were different, the spirit of the story he told was virtually my story. I could identify with every damn thing he said, and that's when I realized what was wrong with me. I'm not crazy. I'm an addict.

CHAPTER 12:
The Road to Rehab & Back Again

During my rehabilitation at Charlotte Treatment Center, I learned things about myself that I had never realized. I dug deep to uncover the sources of the bitterness, the anger, and the uncertainty that had caused my wayward path. I began to understand for the first time why, and how, I had fallen so far. No, I wasn't completely crazy, but then again, would a perfectly sane person make these choices?

The treatment center was in an old elementary school. They put me in a room with two or three other patients the first few days, which was a culture shock to me. I was used to having my own space in my own world. And now I was in unfamiliar and sterile surroundings. In a word, I was just *sad*. And I was so sick. The cold sweats and nightmares dominated my existence day and night. I knew I needed to be there, but coming off of that stuff was harder than I had imagined.

After all those weeks of discovery and therapy, I realized that my problems were a balance between how I was raised, how I had learned to cope with my feelings, and an innate struggle to control my actions once I had begun to use. I learned that alcoholism and addiction *can* be hereditary, which was a concept I had never heard nor considered. Looking back, I don't believe my personal situation was 100%

hereditary, not in the physical or chemical sense. I do believe, however, that it was especially difficult to control my actions once the train began to move down the track. I couldn't have just one drink, one pill, or one line. I had to have it all. Because *all* made my temporary situation go away. *Temporarily.*

I met some interesting people at treatment. And while some of them were instrumental in my recovery, others stood out in a different way. I remember one patient in particular, a man who wore fancy Italian loafers. He arrived at the treatment center in a Cadillac with blood all over him, and an ounce of cocaine in open display on the dashboard. He begged the people at the intake center to take him in. He said his brother was just shot 40 times on a dope deal gone bad, and he didn't have anywhere to go.

Another patient knew the law was after him, and he needed to hide. He was also accused of murdering his wife, and at the time he checked in, they still had not found her. I never asked for details because I didn't really want to know, or most especially be responsible for what I might know.

After I'd been there four or five weeks, I felt the first peace and serenity that I'd felt in years. I walked down to the lake behind the treatment center and watched the ducks swim. I thought, damn, it's nice to be here. The sun is shining, and all I have to do is watch the ducks. Before this day, I was lost. I was freebasing, and it got to the point that I had to have that stuff every day. It's a daily drama because you've got to have that fix. And all I could think of before I got to Charlotte was, "How am I gonna keep up with this and not lose my job?"

And now, here I stood, just a few weeks later, beside the calmness of the lake. I was feeling better, and eating well. I didn't have that jittery feeling. *It was so refreshing.* After what seemed like forever, I began to feel a little human.

I remember well the first day I felt like going outside. They had a basketball goal there, and I picked up a ball at recreation time, which lasted an hour. As I shot around the court, it felt like I was reconnecting with my past, a proverbial 'picking up the ball' once again. And I thought to myself, "I may live yet".

Immediately after treatment, I attended 90 Alcoholics Anonymous or Narcotics Anonymous meetings over 90 days. I was truly focused on living a better life, and taking better care of myself both physically and mentally. I stayed perfectly clean for the next three years, consuming no alcohol or drugs of any kind. I read in my Big Book every night, which is the story of Alcoholics Anonymous and contains their twelve steps. I said a prayer every night, and went to a meeting every day. I visited a drug counselor at Chicopee at least a couple of times a week. I showed up for work early to run and work out. I was on a mission.

I received several promotions at work, and within one year after treatment, I was in a management position. My job was to oversee the efficiency of each shift, and I accomplished those goals faster than anyone had before me. I was on the third shift first, and I thought it would kill me. I had to pull the shades during the day so I could sleep. At the time that I was assigned to that shift, it was the worst performing shift in the company, and I made it number one. Then I did the same with the second shift, and then the first. After my boss was moved up, I took his spot.

I was top dog in three divisions: beaming, extrusion and the warehouse. Then, another company came along and acquired us. They had heard about my management style, and they offered me a bonus of a year's salary to stay on with them. I eagerly accepted the offer, and kept grinding.

About a year later, though, I looked around and almost all the other managers had been fired. Once the new owners got what they wanted from us, they picked us off one by one and brought in college graduates for less money. I could see the writing on the wall.

After 27 years of driving 45 minutes to work each way, I was feeling the stress. The wear and tear on my car, my body, and my sanity, got more intense each year. The traffic was getting heavier, and I was struggling to make it make sense. I was working between Gainesville and Alto, and I was responsible for both crews as well as the construction of a new building. Then the new company brought in someone for me to train. *My own assassin.* That was in 1992, and that's when I woke up and decided to retire early.

I had always dreamed of owning and operating a business from my home, so I decided to build some apartments on the land that I owned. I knew I was paying taxes on a chicken house that was built out of rough cut oak and had good insulation, and I knew it would probably be there forever.

I had already turned another building on the property into a small cabin-like structure that I could rent. So, I took a piece of graph paper and drew out some plans to turn the chicken house into four apartments, and approached Pete Bearden to partner with me and build them. Pete has been a phenomenal friend since my school days, and is an incredible contractor.

At the time, I had $80,000 in my 401K, and I used that money to live on and get all the permits, surveys, and architect drawings completed to build the apartments. I researched and prepared for about two years before the construction began. Once I was ready to go, my Uncle Edgar completed the first phase, which was to clear the land and cut the timber.

The first rental property that was built from the chicken house still exists today. Just a few years later, I would end up with 30 rental units on the property, and every one of the units was occupied within a week after they were completed.

I was so immersed in planning for the apartments and new beginnings that I eventually stopped going to AA and NA meetings. Throughout my treatment in Charlotte, I was indoctrinated to believe that those meetings were essential to maintaining sobriety. And over 50 years later, I'm here to tell you that I agree. In fact, within two weeks after I stopped attending the meetings, I drank my first beer since treatment. And it had devastating consequences.

I drank the beer, and walked toward my 1987 Corvette to head toward home. My friend was riding with me, and he had a bottle of OFC, a Canadian whiskey, in his hand. My friends called it "Odom's Fucking Crazy", which was just one more thing that fed my need for attention.

Before we got into the car, my friend turned around and went back inside to grab a towel. When I asked him why, he said, "I'm going to wrap this jar of OFC in it just in case you wreck us." He was pissed off because I wouldn't let him drive, and I reminded him that he was the one who was drunk, and I had only had one beer.

It was September 1st. I remember the date well because it's Michael's birthday. It was a beautiful day, and the car was spotless. I even had my new jeans on. Everything was looking up, and I thought, "I think I can have a drink again."

We went to the Dawsonville Pool Room and ordered two large cups of ice and water. We got back in the car and drove toward the Y on highway 53, where a roundabout exists today. My friend said he wanted to show me some land. We came down by Bobby Jenkins' house and I threw my hand up to greet Bobby as we passed. I thought to myself, "I'm gonna show him what this thing will do."

There was a little dip in the road, and I pushed the pedal to hit passing gear. But the back wheels kicked in and spun it instead. The car went off the road and over a ridge, flipping upside down as it hit the ridge. We both fell out, and the car landed right side up facing the opposite direction. The next thing I knew, I woke up on my hands and knees with my face buried in the dirt. I was digging in my mouth to get the dirt out so I could breathe.

A local EMT happened to be coming in the opposite direction, and he called for help. The police shut down traffic in both directions on part of the highway to get us to Northeast Georgia Medical Center as quickly as possible. I was told that we both had code blue alerts on the way. I suffered a punctured lung, broken facial bones, broken ribs, a cut spleen, and other internal injuries.

My friend was in a coma for several days with a traumatic brain injury. He ended up having surgery on his brain to release the pressure. Thank God, we both survived, but I don't believe they thought either of us would. The strangest thing about the location of this accident is that it was within feet of where Daddy had wrecked when I was a kid. And the irony of it is that it was known as 'Drunkard Springs'.

Although I had only drunk one beer at the time of the accident, I knew that karma was practically screaming my name. I was headed back down the same treacherous road again, and this time there seemed to be a huge warning sign. Unfortunately, it was a warning that I once again chose to ignore. And it was the beginning of more drinks, more drugs, more accidents, and more losses.

In the next car wreck, another friend of mine was driving. It was raining that day, and the road where we were driving was as slick as glass. I told my friend, "You'd better slow down, and you'd better put on your seatbelt." As soon as he replied, "I never wear a seatbelt", the back end of the car almost lifted up and we swirled around so fast that I saw the car go around once, then twice, almost in slow motion.

Below the road was a creek, surrounded by trees on both sides. I could see where we were headed, and there was no way to avoid the trees. The weight of the front end catapulted the car forward, and it wrapped around a tree, making impact on the driver's side. It was a devastating blow. The impact was so great, and since he wasn't wearing a seatbelt, his body was thrown into mine.

I knew we had to get out of the car immediately, but no car door would open. I shook my friend and told him we needed to get out, that the car could catch on fire. But he didn't move or respond at all. Every time he breathed, blood spurted out everywhere. I knew he didn't have much time. I'm still not sure how I got out of the car that day, but I got out and crawled up to the highway. I laid across the highway, knowing it was my only chance to save him.

Finally, a car stopped and I told them, "Call 911. There's a man bleeding to death down in the creek." I somehow struggled to make my way back to the car, but there was no way I could get him out. The rail was pushed in 17 inches. They had to cut him out of the car. That accident is burned in my memory forever, and I know it caused the PTSD that I still struggle with today.

Although I wasn't under the influence in the first accident, and I wasn't driving in the latter, I knew that those two accidents were a reflection of my choices. In fact, I was constantly reckless. I regularly ran my car off the road, and even reported my BMW stolen three or four times. I just wrecked it and ran. This way, if the law found it, they couldn't blame me for wrecking it or for anything that was in it. That became so routine that the police just sent a wrecker to get it and brought it back to me. I was on a constant high, and I thought nothing could disrupt that. I believed I was invincible.

I also got married again during this time. Although we got along well, this relationship, too, would meet its demise after only a couple of years, and mostly as a result of my actions. I was self-absorbed, and I wasn't ready to share my life with someone again. In fact, I hadn't really been ready for that at any time in my life to that point. When your focus teeters between survival and self-absorption, you hardly have time for anything else.

A second divorce gave me another excuse to continue down the wrong path, and I embraced that opportunity wholeheartedly. The entire time I was building the apartments, I was either high, getting high, or drying out. After the divorce, I got up and cut grass and did business that had to be done. After that, I had nothing to do but party. I stayed messed up pretty much all the time, but with just enough wits about me to function.

I started taking meth, which was cheaper and would keep you going longer. I really thought I had it all together. I had so many systems in place to ensure that I wouldn't get caught. One of those was a stash located in a tall pine tree near my driveway. I had planted a few sprigs of ivy near the base of the tree that I had plucked from my Aunt Ailene's yard. At the time I planted them, I was just looking for a nice ground cover. I wasn't thinking about the fact that they would provide a clever drug cover. But a couple of years later, I realized that ivy stays green year-round, so I came up with the idea to use that tree for my personal drug stash.

I had a retractable clothesline in a round case that I secured about 30 feet up in the tree. The nylon rope inside it was white, but I attached a clear fishing line to the end of it, so when it was retracted, the white nylon was inside the case, but the fishing line couldn't be seen.

My stash was enclosed in a thermos bottle that had rice in it, and secured tightly where the nylon cord met the fishing line. Just one pull of the fishing line, and the thermos full of drugs would come down the tree. Once I had pulled out whatever I wanted, it would easily retract right back up. I tied off the fishing cord on a nail driven into the tree at a level where I could reach it. I used that system so often, there's no telling what's in that tree today.

As the years went by, things got crazier. I was at home one night, really messed up, when I got a call from an acquaintance. He had been locked up at the Dawson County jail, and he was already on probation. He sobbed on the phone and told me how he was still suffering because of his time in Vietnam, and he asked me to come up to the jail at 8:30 that evening to talk about making his bond. He said he felt like he was dying without his pain pills, and I knew what that felt like. In fact, I was on pain pills that very night, and high as a kite. So, I told him I'd be there.

As it was getting closer to 8:30, it began to get darker outside, and it was raining pretty heavily. Unfortunately, none of the cars in my yard would crank. I glanced across the yard at my golf cart, and had a crazy idea. At that moment, I had a one-track mind. I told him I'd be there at 8:30, and I was going to keep my word. So, I jumped on the golf cart and headed up the road for the mile and a half ride to the jail.

The golf cart had a windshield, but the lights wouldn't work because the battery was not fully charged. I rode along the side of the road so I could pull over if I saw anything coming, and I coasted downhill wherever I could. At one point, I noticed a car coming up behind me, so I pulled over behind a cedar tree at the edge of the road. It was an unmarked law car. Still, that didn't deter me, so after it passed, I got back on the road and followed the law car around the courthouse and toward the jail.

The golf cart was getting slower and slower, but I made it to the courthouse parking lot and walked inside. I was wearing a hat that I had recently dyed black, and the dye was dripping all over me, and onto the floor of the lobby. The lady at the reception area looked at me and said, "Oh my God, are you ok?" I said, "Honey, I'm alright. It's just my hat bleeding today." I thought that was humorous, and she laughed, but it dawned on me that I had eight Percocets in my left front pocket, and I knew I could get a DUI if they became suspicious.

I stood up straight and told her that I had come to see someone about making his bond. She told me, "You missed it. That was at 7:30." I was certain, though, that he had told me 8:30. I was disappointed, but now I had to focus on the next problem at hand. I knew I didn't have enough battery left to make it home. I was trying to think of what to say when one of my apartment tenants walked through the lobby door and said, "Gene, come on, we've got a ride for you." It was like a scene from a movie.

I followed him outside without saying anything else to the receptionist. I was so grateful for the ride, but I still needed an explanation for the golf cart in the parking lot. A thousand scenarios were running through my mind, and I was already paranoid. I felt the pills in my pocket, and I sure didn't want to get caught with them, but I also didn't want to waste the pills because they were six dollars each. So, I ate four or five of them and pressed the rest of them down into a mud hole with my shoe.

Then, I walked back in and told the receptionist, "Well, since I can't see him, I've got another issue. I was hauling my golf cart on my trailer, and I got a flat on the trailer and pulled it over at the old jail. I rolled my golf cart down here. Can you keep an eye on it till I can get back tomorrow?" She said, "Sure thing. Don't you worry about it."

I didn't even have a trailer. I left it there for three days because I was afraid to go get it. Finally, I called up a friend and asked him to pick it up on his trailer. Nothing was ever said about it. That night, I was thinking of the time George Jones was arrested for riding his lawn mower under the influence. I felt like an outlaw, but at the same time, I knew it was ridiculously stupid. The whole episode boiled down to my word. I told someone I'd be there, and I did whatever it took.

One of the most memorable moments from my partying days came one Sunday night in the late 80's or early 90's. I was partying with some friends and mentioned that I'd like to have a cold beer. Of course, you couldn't buy beer on Sundays. Then someone mentioned an old man that used to bootleg. He had been shot at a young age, and it had paralyzed him, leaving him bedridden. I used to go to his house as a teenager and knock on the door. When he asked who was at the door, I told him my name and he'd say "Come on in, little Odom. I've got beer, red liquor (which was known as government liquor), truck driver pills, whatever you need."

When my friends suggested we get beer from him that Sunday, I replied, "No, he's dead." But they insisted that he wasn't. To my surprise, not only was he not dead, he was still living in the same place and was still in the business. It had been 33 years.

We drove there that night, and knocked on the door. He asked who it was and I yelled, "Little Odom!" He said, "Goddamn, Little Odom, come on in. Where the hell have you been?" I said, "I thought you died!" Everything was exactly the same. The refrigerator was in the same place, the beer was in the same location, and he still sold beer, liquor and pills.

After that night, I began to think that his bootleg house might be another great stash place for me. So, I approached him and said, "I know you've always dealt with a little of this and that. What if I had something I wanted to stash? I would keep it outside, and come up here for beer and get something from my little stash. I can give you $100 a week, and if anything happens to you, I'll claim it. And you know as well as I do, they don't want to lock you up for bootlegging. They don't want to take care of you. What do you think?" And just like wash, rinse, and repeat, he shouted, "Goddamn, Odom, when are we gonna start?"

For years, I'd visit him and get beer, get an ounce of my coke, and head on out. What better place than a bootlegger's house to keep your dope? The law thought I was going in for beer, and I came out with beer.

My differences with the law would prompt the next big idea. It's one I'm not proud of today, but up until then, I had always been told that the law is nothing but trouble. And good for nothing. I hated the law because they took my Daddy away from me for four years, when I needed him most. It changed him, and he was different when he got out. I resented that, but today, I feel very differently. I respect them now.

Back then, it occurred to me that if the law stopped me with drugs, I had to have a way to dispose of them cleverly. So, I hired a mechanic to weld a header pipe under the car and install a rubber plug that looked like a wiring harness. It opened up to an empty hole. If I was pulled over, all I had to do was remove the plug and drop the drugs through the hole just before my car came to a stop. If I timed it right, the law car would be resting right on top of the drugs. I used this hole method at least three times.

One of those times was when I was pulled over on Burnt Stand Road in Dahlonega. As soon as the officer met my car on the road, she turned around. I was totally sober, but I did have drugs on me. I dropped 2-3 eight balls of dope into the hole, and it hit the ground below. It should have ended up under the officer's car or near it by the time we came to a stop.

When she approached the window, I asked her why she had pulled me over. She said I was speeding and swerving, but I knew I wasn't. Then she told me that I was in a high traffic area for drugs, and she needed to search the car. I told her she couldn't do that without a search warrant.

She immediately called for a K-9 unit, and they literally showed up within 60 seconds. I knew they were waiting for me. The dog went under the vehicle on the passenger side, and stayed and stayed. The officer appeared frustrated, and finally said, "The dog didn't hit on anything, so I'm gonna let you go." And I just looked at her and said, "What made you think I had drugs?" She never answered.

When I got back home, one of the eight balls had landed on top of the transmission and it was still there. The only thing I can figure is that the grease masked the smell of the dope, and that's why the dogs stayed so long in that spot.

Although those moments came with a lot of bravado, they also came with a lot of sacrifice. My addiction contributed to my problems and became more problems. Every bad choice I made just made things worse. And every time I tried to get off the drugs, especially the pain pills, I felt all that pain from the inside out. It might be during a time when things are going really good, or a low time, like when someone dies.

One of those times was in 2002, when I found out Mama had cancer. Five days after her diagnosis, she died. I was in complete shock. We had been eating breakfast together every morning for the last few years, and suddenly, all of that was just a memory.

When the doctors told us that we had to make a decision about taking her off of life support, I told them they were crazy. I said, "She's only been here four days, and we don't even know what's wrong." That's when they told me that she was eaten up with cancer. So, I left the hospital searching for more answers, and went to her doctor's office. He was on vacation, and I tried to press the staff for information, but they gave me none.

The next day, they just pulled the plug. There was no further explanation. I still wonder about the way that was handled, and how something could happen that quickly. She might have known about the cancer earlier and chose not to say anything, but we'll never know. It was all very surreal.

The day she died, I didn't know what to do. I picked up a jug of liquor and went to a friend's house and asked if I could sit by his pool. I couldn't handle the pressure. The truth is, I never did learn how to handle things like that.

I continued down a treacherous road for two more decades. Sometimes I got better, and sometimes things got worse. One of the worst was the disconnection between me and my son, Michael. In hindsight, I know that I failed him in many ways. I failed to see how my actions both influenced and harmed him. I was in a constant state of something besides myself most of the time we were together. I made choices that put us both in difficult and impossible situations, despite my intentions. I can only speak from my side of the equation, and I realize the part I played in the outcome. The fracture in our relationship is one of my greatest regrets.

Another of those low points was when Daddy died. I was stressed and didn't want to accept the fact that he was dying. All I could think about was the pain. By this time, in 2017, there had been a lot of pain, and it was moments like these that brought it back to the surface. After his death, I collapsed near the apartments with a jug of liquor in each hand.

The paramedics took me to Peachtree Rehab Center in Atlanta, where I woke in an empty room on a concrete floor. I beat on the door, begging them to let me out. I told them I was freezing and just needed a blanket. They were not concerned, and did nothing to comfort me. And I guess I can't blame them. If a rehab center was like the Taj Mahal, I guess you'd never learn from your mistakes, would you?

There were so many patients there, ranging from relatively calm addicts like me to violent criminals. I witnessed bloody fights that scared me to death, so I did my best to sit in a corner and remain quiet. When I was finally released into a long-term rehabilitation program, they drove me straight to the apartments to check in. They went through my suitcase, and repeatedly told me they were the boss for the next few weeks, and I knew they would be.

The long-term center was in an unfamiliar and questionable area of town, and I just couldn't imagine staying there. As soon as I checked in, I made my bed, but instead of going out back to play chess or cards with the other patients, I went out the front door and ran and ran and ran. I was soaking wet with sweat, had no money, and no belongings except the clothes on my back. I finally asked someone to use their phone and called for a ride home. I'll never forget that feeling of desperation.

When I got back home, I knew I still needed help if I was going to get off the pain pills. I was doing better, but the pills had a grip on me that I knew I couldn't overcome by myself. I was taking OxyContin, made from opium, the same natural substance used to make heroin. And it's the hardest thing I've ever battled.

Day after day, I thought I'd get a little better and I didn't. I had vivid nightmares that ended with me screaming and jumping in the middle of the bed. They made me so sick. I had just about given up on myself, and knew I had to check in somewhere for my third treatment. I knew I had to make it work.

I went to another rehab center in Helen called The Black Bear. I completed their 30-day program, and that did get me back on my feet. Since then, I have done well. I wish I could say I conquered those demons and never allowed them to see light again, but that would be a lie. I have taken large steps forward, and small steps backward at times. But altogether, I have managed to keep the demons at bay and live a sober life.

When you're doing drugs, you don't realize they're like cancer. They eat away at you ever so slowly. Slow enough that you don't realize the damage that's taking place each day, and fast enough that you can't see the end coming.

When you're in the midst of it, it's like your brain telling you that you're hungry. It's a simple answer. You eat. Likewise, if you feel uncomfortable, afraid or anxious, you'll crave whatever it takes to get those feelings to subside. And if you have a propensity for addiction, and you have something nearby that will help numb the pain, you're probably gonna use it.

Being addicted means you're suffering all the time. But, after you've been sober for a couple of months, you get a serene feeling. There's a peace that comes over you, like God just draped a blanket over you. All those insecurities just go away. You realize that you don't have to do this to yourself. You're free. You don't have any obligations that you can't handle. And all the insecurities and drama are gone. It's like a new life.

And yet, down the road you may hit a slump and your brain will convince you that you deserve to be high. It comes on so subtly. No one except another addict can understand how that happens. And then just like that, you find yourself still digging the hole, 60 years later. Only this time, it's harder to get out.

I WAS THERE
Michael's Memories

Earlier in this chapter, Daddy mentions the fragmentation in our relationship. We've been down some rough roads together, for sure. When Tonya asked me to contribute to the book, I really didn't hesitate at all. You'd have to understand the dynamic in our family. Just because there is tension, it doesn't mean there isn't love. And just because there were many chaotic and even catastrophic events throughout the years, it doesn't mean there wasn't laughter.

I told Tonya I would be glad to share a few stories with you that make me shake my head and chuckle to this day. And yes, Daddy has agreed that these events actually happened, just as they are written here.

One afternoon I was playing softball inside the empty chicken house with some friends. We hit the ball up into the ceiling, and down came a container full of Quaaludes. I was around eleven years old. I had already discovered the pot in the chicken house by this time. And those days marked the beginning of the tumultuous journey that transformed his life and mine.

I lived with him (or near him) for the better part of about eighteen years. I could have run a Fortune 500 company for less than what I went through during those years. I felt like I was trying to keep everything together while he was just acting like a fool. And trust me when I say that it was an everyday thing for a while.

One event that comes to mind was the day he got lost on the river. It was getting dark, and some of Daddy's friends came to me and told me that he had gone down the river in a canoe earlier that afternoon and wasn't back yet. They were getting worried, and they thought someone should look for him.

My first thought was, "Did it occur to you to tell me sooner? Or go look for him yourself?" But you have to know, that wasn't the way things were done when I was living with Daddy. Most of the time, the responsibility for such things landed squarely on me, and if I'm being honest, it sucked. After calling everyone I knew and searching a couple of places around town, me and a friend grabbed one of our canoes and headed to the river. We traveled the same route that he took, and searched with a spotlight, looking for an overturned canoe or any sign of him along the river banks.

It was after daylight when we finally got off the river. I was so worried, and headed back home to see if there was any word about him. When I got back to the house, there he was...in bed, after having breakfast at Waffle House. He was just lying there, 'chillin' like a villain'.

When Grandpa came to live with him, I thought things might improve because he had more responsibility. Unfortunately, things got even worse. Many nights, I found myself putting both of them to bed.

Even Grandpa would occasionally get out of control, like the time he drove his old 1974 Mustang II up to Dawsonville. You've got to understand, Grandpa was 75 years old when he came to live with Dad, and he was so feeble that he could barely walk. Both of his feet needed surgery, so driving was completely off limits. Or at least we thought it was.

The Mustang had been parked down at the apartments, and Daddy just left the key in it. We didn't think there would be any trouble. In fact, we'd had a discussion about the fact that he should not be driving, and Grandpa agreed. But one day Daddy looked down toward the parking lot and the car was gone. Moments later, a police cruiser pulled into the driveway with Grandpa in the back. He had made a beer run, and then ran out of gas on his way back home.

The officer who brought him home was really kind and understanding. I'm sure he thought he was dealing with a feeble, elderly man and he felt sorry for him. Luckily, he ignored the beer in the car, and just said, "I'm gonna do him a favor this time."

When Grandpa ran out of gas, he must have just sat there drinking, because by the time they picked him up, he was dog drunk. As soon as he stumbled out of the police car, he stood up as straight as he could and told the officer, "I'd have outrun your ass if I'd had anything that could run." Grandpa was spirited, and on one hand, it was refreshing. On the other, it was hell.

And speaking of hell, for most of you, the holidays are probably a joyful and peaceful time. But with Daddy, it was like walking on pins and needles. That's because you could count on the craziness to happen every single year. He had always loved Elvis, and he played his Christmas albums at the start of every Thanksgiving. He even had an Elvis voice on his answering machine. "This is not The King...it's only Gene", was what the message said. The song Blue Christmas was playing in the background. He usually kept that on his machine long past the holidays.

One particular Christmas, he decided that decorating the golf cart that he used for the apartments simply wasn't enough. After all, he couldn't drive it just anywhere. So, he came up with the idea of velcroing a dancing Santa Claus to the hood of Grandpa's old red pickup. It was about eight inches tall, and when you made a noise (like clapping your hands), Santa danced and sang.

Daddy was thrilled with this idea, and worked to attach that Santa Claus to the truck like it was his job. But since it was the holidays and all, of course that wasn't quite enough. So, he added a little extra holiday flair by gluing an actual wine glass to the top of the truck cab near the driver's door.

Now, picture this. A grown man, driving through Dawsonville, with a dancing Santa and wine glass glued to the truck. You'd think this would be a one-time thing, right? But no. Santa fell off several times, but Daddy just glued him back on and kept running all his errands in that truck. Every single day for about a month.

When the velcro came loose, he tried weather strip adhesive. One section of the hood was nothing but solid glue from reapplying it each time it fell off.

One day he was headed down the road to show some kids the dancing Santa Claus when it fell off the hood for at least the fifteenth time. Daddy pulled off the road and attempted to put it back on using

3M adhesive spray. When he attempted to spray it, though, he realized that his sprayer was clogged, so he decided to make another genius move and stick a knife through the bottom of the can to allow the glue to squirt out that way.

When he did that, it started spraying everywhere, so he just dropped it onto the ground. By that time, glue had gotten on everything. The grill, the bumper, his shoes. He said he didn't think anything about it, he just had one mission in mind, and that was gluing Santa back on.

When it still didn't stick well, he decided to light a match and heat the glue a little. *Now, you and I both know what happens when you set fire to adhesive glue*, but apparently, he didn't connect the dots that day. On a side note, we had just been through a dry spell throughout the entire county, with water rotation regulations and warnings all over the news.

As soon as the flame came in contact with the glue, he heard a 'whoof', and the fire spread. It caught his pants leg on fire, and he found a jacket and beat the fire out of his pants first. He then turned back toward the truck, and luckily, he was able to put out the rest of the fire before it spread.

When I saw the truck after that incident, I couldn't believe it. It had charred the entire grill and halfway up the hood. But he was proud to say that he got that damn Santa Claus back on and went on his 'merry' way to show some kids.

That wasn't the end of his 'fiery' days, though. Daddy had a beautiful 1987 green BMW that he had bought in Cumming. One day I noticed that he had painted the tires and BBS wheels a bright, fluorescent orange color. That was puzzling enough, but the next day, as I was passing by the house, I saw that the car was on fire, and it was parked right underneath the power lines.

The fire department was there, and I pulled in to make sure he was okay. Daddy was pacing back and forth, just mumbling to himself. He was acting crazy as hell, out of his mind. I'm not sure what he told them or what they surmised, but the fire department just put out the fire and headed back down the road.

For about a two-year period, he stayed drunk and played the drums almost every night. He put a set of drums in the corner of his dining room, and he would often just mumble into the microphone and beat the drums with no rhythm at all. People were running in and out of the house at all hours, and drugs were everywhere. I couldn't do anything *for* him...or *with* him.

When things got really bad, he would agree to go to the hospital in an attempt to dry out and get some relief. During one of those visits, he tested positive for 15 drugs, including marijuana, heroin, alcohol, meth, Xanax, Valium, and OxyContin.

Yes, it was complete chaos, but we had a lot of good times, too. Like the time he tossed a hat about 30 feet, from the living room into the kitchen, and it landed perfectly on my head. I never smiled or anything. I just gave him a thumbs-up. We have a video of that somewhere.

I have hundreds of stories, most of which I'll never tell, and we're probably all better off if I don't. When I have a chance to reflect on all of it, I know two things. I'd never want to go through that again. And I still love my Daddy. Despite all the hurt and disappointment that runs between us, I still love him. One day I believe we'll understand each other better, and maybe this book is one small step for me today...and one giant leap for the future.

CONCLUSION:
Repairing & Reuniting

Throughout most of this book you've heard some pretty damning and controversial things about my family, especially Mama and Daddy. I wish I could say they were not true. But one thing is for sure; the twists and turns of life have surprised the weakest and the strongest among us, and I am no exception. So, I'd like to share with you a few of the great adventures and revelations we had together in their later years. Some of those were a result of the continued pattern of addiction, and others would be considered almost normal.

JANET:

I'd like to begin with my sister, Janet. When I got married right out of high school, she was still living at Ethel's. Shortly afterward, she began dating a man named Phillip, and they got married and moved to Talking Rock, Georgia. We only stayed in touch intermittently after that. We saw each other when Janet visited Mama, or when we occasionally visited them, which was just a handful of times a year.

Janet seemed to be living the life and doing fine at first, but at a young age, she started having migraine headaches. She made multiple trips to doctors and hospitals in search of help. That's when her doctor began prescribing her pain pills. Then another doctor did the same. And another.

She made no secret of the fact that she didn't approve of my lifestyle. She looked down on me for doing 'street drugs'. She was convinced that if the doctor prescribed the drugs, they were fine. She never changed her view on that. Over the years that followed, the drugs she was prescribed would actually cause more problems than they solved.

Janet was a private person, but she was also in great denial about the relationship between the drugs and her failing health. Whenever she did visit, she put on a brave face. She was dressed up, wearing lots of jewelry, and driving one of her fancy cars, like her Corvette or Z-28. She was showing one side to the world, and hiding the other behind the walls of her home. She was eccentric and materialistic in ways, but soft and kind underneath it all.

I know that one of the biggest regrets in her life was being unable to have children, and I can imagine how that added to the pain she experienced, probably in a massive way. I believe she would have been a very good mother.

She was always sweet to Tonya and Michael, showing up to quite a few of their ball games, school events and parades. She even drove them through Homecoming and sports parades in her cars. The kids loved the attention, and they loved her.

I believe if Janet and I were raised under different circumstances, we might have been very close. We just simply didn't know each other. As strange as that sounds, it's a truth that jumps off the pages of my old photo albums every time I pull one out. It's like looking at a stranger, wondering what happened and why I don't remember her. The photographs show innocence and smiles, but I have no recollection of those days or moments at all.

I do, however, remember the end, and how it provided a clarity about addiction that I believe everyone should know. *It doesn't matter where the drugs come from.* It doesn't matter whether they come from the streets or the pharmacy. They all have the ability to kill. And at the age of 55, they took Janet's life. One of the last times I saw her, she told me she was "going in for a little surgery". In actuality, they removed part of her colon. All of those prescription medications had caused irreparable damage to her stomach and intestines.

She called me a week before she died. I could tell when she was taking medication, and she seemed to be that day for sure. She said, "Bro, I'm thinking of moving back home. Do you have an apartment available?" I said, "Yes, I have a few that are empty. Just come on over and pick the one you want." This was exactly a week before she died, and I never saw her or heard from her again.

Janet died of addiction, and I understand better than most how it can happen. She, too, was just trying to cope with what we went through. She was trying to numb the pain. She may have gone through more than I did. Honestly, I have very little recollection of her. It was almost like she didn't exist. I don't understand it, and sometimes it haunts me. It was just me taking care of me, and her taking care of her, and we both got lost.

MAMA:

Just a few short years after I got married to Kay, Mama moved onto the same land near me, and she lived within walking distance from me until the day she died. She really loved Kay, and they had some fun adventures together, a few at my expense. One time they wrecked my green Toyota truck and told me that someone had let a grocery cart full of groceries get away from them and it hit the truck. Over 30 years later, I'd find out that they hit a culvert.

There was one incident I recall which was typical of my childhood and yet at the same time, I still laugh hysterically about it today. It happened during the construction of the apartments, which were built between my house and Mama's. I frequently hired Mama to do things around the house like raking the yard and trimming the shrubs. It helped give her a little spending money, and also gave her something to do to keep her active. She would often invite her good friend along to help out.

On the day of the incident, she was doing some work for me, and had been in and out of the house, and unfortunately, nipping some of my white liquor. It wasn't something that she did often, but when she did, I can assure you that nothing good came from it.

I was at work that day, but there were some construction workers on the property, and this is pretty much how they tell the story. Mama was helping me varnish some wood inside the old egg house that we were turning into a rental unit. I stored a lot of stuff in there that I didn't have room for at the house, including seasonal items.

Mama and her friend came out of the egg house, both wearing Halloween masks. They were made of rubber, the kind you pulled over your head. They got into my truck with the masks on, and cranked it. I had a driveway on each side of the house, so if you exited one driveway and turned onto Highway 9, the other driveway entrance was just about 50 yards away.

The workers said Mama floored the gas pedal and went from one driveway, out into the street, and into the other without ever touching the brakes. When she started to make the final turn onto the paved part of the driveway that led up to the garage, she slammed into a tree. They said it was a hard hit. In fact, hard enough to total the truck.

The workers ran to see if both women were OK, and they said Mama got out of the truck stumbling a little, but waved them off. She was still wearing the mask, and blood was dripping steadily from underneath it. They both just walked away from the truck and down the hill toward her trailer.

When I got home later that day, I saw the truck rammed into the tree. I panicked, because I didn't know what had happened, and I immediately asked the workers. I got this whole story from them. I couldn't believe it.

I didn't see Mama for several weeks after that. Every time I went down to check on her or try to talk to her, she wouldn't come to the door. I just left the truck wrapped around the tree for weeks, hoping she would walk up to the house and talk to me about it. She was ashamed of the incident, I'm sure. And honestly, I didn't know whether to cringe or chuckle. When she finally did answer the door, she acted like nothing ever happened, and never mentioned it again.

As the years went by, we spent a lot of time together. She was never one to cook too much, but occasionally she'd make black-eyed peas, soup beans and cornbread. And she loved to drink coffee. As hot as you could stand it, any time of the day or night.

My fondest memories were in her last few years, when we had breakfast together every morning. She had struggled with arthritis most of her life, and in those final years it got much worse. I called her every morning and asked her if she had a good night. If she told me she had a pretty good night, she'd offer to fix biscuits and gravy for us. But if she replied that she'd had a rough one, I just said, "I'll run to Dawsonville and pick something up. I'll be right down." And I usually picked up biscuits and gravy from Dairy Queen. During those mornings, we became as close as we ever were.

When I think about my memories of her, I remember most of all the pride she took in her home. She owned a double wide trailer, and every inch of it was cleaned to perfection, all the time. The yard was always pristine, too. She didn't have the brick house anymore, but she took care of what she did have.

In her final years, she also lost her desire to drink and stopped altogether. She was a changed person, and that was nice to see. It was like dealing with a totally different human being, which was a tremendous relief. She had become content living alone, and really didn't want anyone staying with her.

In 2001, her brother, Herman, was murdered. He was beaten to death with a wooden stick outside of his apartment in Dahlonega, Georgia. He was such a kind and gentle soul. He was quiet, so quiet you'd almost forget he was around. He helped anyone who needed a hand, from giving them a ride to picking up groceries. The murder was senseless, and though they arrested the killer, he was declared mentally incompetent to stand trial, and was let go. That affected Mama terribly, and I felt so sorry for her because she had lost two brothers to murder. I worried that it might tip the scales for her to drink again, but she never did.

Sometimes I recall those days with great fondness, and other times with melancholy. I know she was suffering, but I didn't know just how much until those final four days in the hospital. I honestly believed she just had a bad case of arthritis. She had taken gold shots for years to help with the pain. Sometimes they seemed to help, and sometimes they didn't. But she never mentioned that it was cancer. I first learned that from the staff at the hospital. Maybe she was ashamed to tell me because she had never stopped smoking, so she didn't want to be judged. Or maybe she had just found out herself. I'll probably never know the answer to that.

But in those final days, I certainly did not expect that I'd never see her again. I was in disbelief when they told me they were planning to pull the plug. Like a train had come out of nowhere and I was standing on the tracks with no ability to see or hear what was coming.

And I have often wondered since then whether I would have changed anything about our final years together. I honestly don't think I would. She knew I loved her and would do anything to help her, and she was always there for me. It was not the typical closeness between a mother and child, but it was the best we'd had. I was grateful to get to know her more and spend time with her. But there was still a child's longing for a loving relationship that I would never come to know.

People have asked me how I forgave her. Truthfully, I didn't consciously think about forgiving her. In fact, I'm not even sure how it came about. It was just an organic thing that happened over time. I'm convinced that Mama loved me in the best way she knew how. Perhaps the only way.

DADDY:

Daddy and his wife, Mamie, lived right on the edge of Buford Dam in Cumming, in a modest little white house with a fenced yard. Mamie told him what to do and when to do it. And as a result, we only saw him once or twice a year for thirty years.

When Mamie passed away, there was no one left to take care of him. He wanted to continue living in their home, but he had been neglecting his health for many years. He had bone spurs on both feet, and when he walked, all he could really do was shuffle his feet. One day he fell at home and it messed up his face pretty badly. The neighbors called me and told me that he was just sitting at home drinking Ensure and beer, and taking pills. I knew he had been taking Xanax and pain pills for his legs and feet, but I had no idea that he had been taking it for almost twenty years.

That's when he came to live with me, at the age of 75. This was a bittersweet time for sure. We went through a lot together. I helped him get off all of the pills, and made sure he had surgery on both of his feet. He really was a pitiful sight, but I learned quickly not to be foolish about the old man.

For instance, one evening I was headed into town, and got into the car inside the garage (which faced the sliding glass door off the living room). He had told me for days that he didn't feel well, and was unable to even walk.

As I was backing out of the garage, I glanced forward first and thought I saw something moving quickly across the hallway. And when I say quickly, it was sort of like a bullet. I said to my friend who was in the car with me, "Did you see that?" She replied, "Yep, it looked like something ran across the hallway."

I promptly got out of the car and went inside. As I entered Daddy's bedroom, he was sitting in bed holding a half-gallon of white liquor in his hand. Earlier that day I had placed the liquor behind the hallway door. He must have heard the sound of the glass jug as it scraped across the floor. He remembered that, and took the first opportunity to grab it as soon as he thought I had left the house. I never would have thought he was capable of walking that far, let alone practically sprinting.

It was moments like those that made me recall the bad days. And sometimes I also behaved like a vengeful child, like the day I was driving the BMW with Daddy in tow, and I decided that I wanted to show him that I had balls as big as his. I could drive fast cars, too. I got up to 145 miles an hour. The front end was starting to dart around with the wind, and that's when Daddy said, "that's enough". I felt a strong urge to let him know I could handle anything he could handle. It was a moment I'm not proud of, but at the time, I felt it served its purpose.

Daddy lived with me for about five years total, including my time in Dahlonega after I moved in with Cheryl. She was very kind to Daddy, and helped to take care of him even while working full time. I appreciate that dedication and admire her for it still today.

He loved to sit outside on the porch at both houses, and would watch the traffic and squirrels for hours. He even named the squirrels, and would tell me about their escapades with the exuberance of a child.

We had good days and bad. And if I'm being truly honest, they were mostly bad. Anyone who has taken care of an aging parent or grandparent knows the plight. It's rewarding and full of love, but also riddled with frustration. Daddy's frustrations came from his lack of motivation to walk. No matter what we said or did, he wouldn't exert the energy to exercise his legs and keep himself mobile. We took care of him as long as we could physically do it, and then he moved to a nearby nursing home.

His last few years were spent with the staff waiting on him hand and foot. He enjoyed eating candy and loved the attention from the female nurses. He liked having visitors, but seemed content most of the time, regardless of whether he was chatting with a neighbor or spending time alone.

A few years after he went into the nursing home, Daddy had a mild stroke. It didn't really affect his movements, but it did impact his speech. Although it became increasingly harder to understand him, we still communicated pretty well.

One of his favorite things in life was to ride in my 1973 Scout. He had been for many rides in it with the top down. We used to ride to Ruby Tuesday's sometimes for salmon and his one allotted glass of wine. He loved riding in it no matter where he was going.

During one of our last good encounters, I came to visit him in the Scout. I rolled his wheelchair up to the lobby of the nursing home so he could see outside, and I had parked the Scout right up front. He was feeble, and his face was thin and gaunt looking. We both knew he didn't have much time left.

He didn't say a word. He just looked sad, and muttered the word "wide". I knew that meant he wanted to go for a ride. I went back inside and talked the staff into letting him take a ride with me. We set him up in the seat so he wouldn't slump over, and we rode to the Pool Room to get him a vegetable plate. Then we rode down to the house and parked near the first apartments I'd built, which looked out over an open field. I still shudder when I recall that moment, because we both knew it would be the last time he'd ever be 'home'.

His final hours were some of the hardest of my life. I went off the deep end when Daddy was dying. Once again, I couldn't handle the reality of what was happening. I couldn't face the thought of losing him, especially after we had spent so much time together. It wasn't as though he was lost, and then found. It was like I was still finding him. Still searching for something to ground myself.

And as life will do, it reminds you of humanity. And humanity could not exist without humor, which reared its head within his final hours inside Gold City Nursing Home. The nurses visited his room one by one. They were all genuinely tearful, and shared so many memories of caring for him, anxious to let us know that they had some very lively moments inside those walls.

At one time, three nurses were standing outside of his room, and one of them mentioned, "Every time I tried to change his clothes or feed him, he grabbed a handful." We were stunned a little, but knew exactly what she was trying to say. And then the second nurse chimed in. "Yes, me too. He used to smack me on the butt." And then the third followed suit with a similar tale. Apparently, he had more adventures than I knew.

I'll never forget asking him one day, "Daddy, if you could make liquor again, would you do it?" Without a hint of hesitation, he looked me squarely in the eye and said "Yep". Unlike Mama, he never lost the desire to drink. He would have drunk as much as you'd have given him.

I've heard that you can't change the stripes on a tiger, and Daddy is living proof of that statement. He's also living proof that behind every man, strong or struggling, righteous or rebel, there is indeed a human worthy of respect in his own right.

The End

ABOUT GENE

Born on December 10, 1947, Glenn Eugene Odom entered a life of complexity, uncertainty, and chance. His Daddy was a moonshiner in the hills of North Georgia, and his Mama was a housewife who occasionally participated in the family business as well. They were poor most of the time, as the moonshine business was a feast or famine enterprise. And when both of your parents were alcoholics, the feast certainly never lasted long.

Gene was an exuberant child, adventure pouring through his veins. He remembers racing around school throughout an entire recess with a piece of notebook paper taped to his chest with a number on it. His endless energy was infectious to others, and he was a beloved child. Among his happier memories, he recalls the time his Daddy returned from a still after six months with enough money to buy some land, build a house and buy a new car. For the first time, it instilled in him a sense of hope and security. But in just a few short years, that hope and wealth faded as furiously as it had arrived.

His Daddy was sent to prison, and suddenly they had no money or food, and they were losing their home. He went to visit him one Sunday, and asked him, "If I dig out from under the house and put a still under there, reckon we could save the house?". He said, "Son, you can try it but I don't think that will work." Gene's young survivalist mentality set in and he took a small metal shovel and a Radio Flyer wagon and began to dig and haul. He was just fourteen years old. It took him weeks, but he dug a hole so large that a Volkswagen would almost fit inside. And then one night in a moment of despair, realization set in. It would never work.

Throughout the turbulent times of his youth, however, he found one undeniable saving grace and passion...basketball. As he entered high school, it was unusual for a freshman player to be invited to join the Varsity team, and he earned the spot. He went on to become known throughout the state of Georgia as one of the finest players of his time. His senior year, he averaged 31 points per game (prior to three point lines), ranking 7th in the state. He was offered college scholarships, and was hopeful that his life was finally headed in the right direction. And then came a dilemma of his own making. He and his high school girlfriend were expecting a baby.

Gene knew he had to do the right thing, and although he wished for the time that it had been different, he has never uttered regret about the decision to get married and care for his new family. In the years ahead, they would purchase their first home and have another child as he spent 27 years working at a manufacturing plant in Gainesville, Georgia. Everything was going well once again, until a seemingly benign choice would prove to rock the foundation of his family and future. It all began with gathering, cleaning, and selling milk jugs...and progressed to marijuana, cocaine, and methamphetamine. The poor choices multiplied, and the turbulence continued.

Today, Gene lives in Dahlonega, Georgia with his wife, Cheryl. He and his daughter spent two years conducting phone sessions, meetings, and research in preparation for *The Raising of a Rebel*. In the book, Gene shares the twelve turning points in his life from the perspective of a child of alcoholics. His hope is that others, especially youth, will gain wisdom from his mistakes and inspiration from his recovery.

ABOUT TONYA

Tonya Eberhart is a speaker, bestselling author, and *Branding Agent to Business Stars*. She grew up in Dawsonville, a small North Georgia town best known for making moonshine and fueling the auto racing industry.

After she graduated from high school, her wild ambitions landed her a theatre scholarship at a local community college, followed by a move to Tallahassee, Florida to attend the renowned theatre program at Florida State University. But she was soon to discover that she was out of place in the quirky, eccentric world of theatre. So, she used her acting skills for a more suitable purpose—vacuum cleaner sales.

While selling vacuums door to door to pay for her education, she happened upon the home of a radio station engineer who recommended her for a sales position, which began an eighteen-year journey in radio. During this time, Tonya observed business owners who were featured in their own advertising and positioned as local celebrities in their market. She was intrigued by this, and determined to help others achieve that level of success. She hand-picked clients whom she felt she could turn into the next radio star, and invited them into the studio to record their own commercials. This was just the beginning of helping many business owners to build their personal brands across multiple marketing platforms.

Several years and many successful brands later, she founded BrandFace®, the only comprehensive personal brand building system across the globe. It consists of step by step branding programs, a book series, and a speaking series that is designed to help serious professionals differentiate themselves. Their mantra is, *"People don't do business with a logo. They do business with a person."*

Tonya's first published book was a collaboration with her daughter, Kati Eberhart, called *Kati's Journey (One Teen's Journey to Japan)*, and is the first interactive book written by a U.S. teen. It shares Kati's passion for Asian culture and chronicles their trip to Japan in 2012, featuring accounts from both mother and daughter. After founding BrandFace® in 2013, she has also authored four books on the subject of personal branding designed to help business owners, entrepreneurs, home improvement professionals, and real estate professionals.

Her sixth book, *The Raising of a Rebel*, is a memoir of her father, Gene Odom. It's a story of his heartbreaking struggles and the effects of his upbringing as a child of alcoholics.

Tonya is known for her exclusive personal branding concepts that help people to share their authentic story and unveil their inner star for massive recognition and riches. Her favorite statement is, "A great brand doesn't just change the way others see you. It changes the way you see *yourself*."

She travels the world for both business and pleasure, with her home base in Jefferson, Georgia. She relies on her children (Kati and Chuck) to keep her grounded, humbled, and constantly laughing. And her partner in business and in life (Michael Carr), is the man whom she says completes her own story every single day.

PLEASE LEAVE US A REVIEW

We truly appreciate the time you took to read this book. If it moved you in any way, we'd be honored if you'd consider leaving a review for us on Amazon.

Simply visit Amazon.com and enter the book title, *The Raising of a Rebel*. Click on the book, and on that page, you'll see an area to leave a review. Please keep in mind that you will need to be logged in to Amazon in order to complete the review.

Thank you so much for your consideration!

Made in the USA
Columbia, SC
24 October 2024

45025514R00100